The Bicycle Repair Book

The
Bicycle Repair
Book

The NEW Complete Manual of Bicycle Care

Rob van der Plas

Illustrated by the author

BICYCLE BOOKS
FROM
MBI Publishing Company

Second, fully updated edition, 1993
Third printing of this edition, 1995
Printed in U.S.A.

Cover design:
Kent Lytle, Lytle Design
Front cover photograph taken at *American Cyclery*, San Francisco

Bicycles for some of the text photographs courtesy *Moutain Avenue*, San Fransico; *A Bicycle Odyssey*, Sausalito; *Gazelle*, Holland; *Fahrradgesellschaft*, Germany. Some other equipment courtesy Shimano Europe and Sachs.

Cataloging in Publication Data
van der Plas, Robert, 1938 —
Bicycles and Bicycling, handbooks and manuals
I. Title
II. Authorship
Library of Congress Catalog Card No. 92-83822
ISBN 0-933201-055-9

Rob van der Plas is a professional engineer and a lifelong cyclist who has written about the subject for specialized magazines since 1975. During the late 70s and early 80s he wrote several general bicycle books for Dutch, German and British publishers.

In 1984 his *Mountain Bike Book*, the first book on the subject of what was then a new breed of bicycles, was published by Velo Press, which later became Bicycle Books. Since then Bicycle Books has published at least one new book by him each year, starting with the first edition of *The Bicycle Repair Book* in 1985. His other books include *Roadside Bicycle Repair, Mountain Bike Maintenance, The Bicycle Touring Manual, The Bicycle Racing Guide* and *Bicycle Technology*.

This book is devoted to bicycle repair and maintenance only. It includes general and step-by step instructions for handling just about every maintenance job you will ever encounter. It covers not only the latest and the most fashionable equipment sold today (althought that is ialso treated at length) but also older and less common products. I have done that after due deliberation, since many readers will not only want to work on bikes that are brand new out of the showroom, but also on machines that are a couple of years old, or even machines that have been around for decades. I feel we should not think of the bicycle as a throwaway fashion product, but as a durable good that, when treated correctly, will last a lifetime.

Like all other books published by Bicycle Books, this title is sold in the U.S. and i n other English-speaking countries. In each of those countries some things are called by different names. Thus, what Americans refer to as a wrench is known as a spanner in the U.K., a crankset is a chain-set, and there are a myriad of words that are spelled differently — center versus centre, aluminum versus aluminium, tire versus tyre. Although American spelling is used, I have made every effort to clarify terms that may not be clear in one culture or the other, giving English "translations" for words that differ by more than the spelling alone.

In these pages, I have also tried to include all the information that seems relevant to the subject of bicycle maintenance and repair. I describe the methods I use myself, based on 40 years of hands-on experience, but I know there are other ways of doing some of the jobs described. If you, the cyclist, know of better ways to tackle certain jobs, I would appreciate hearing from you.

Send any comments you may have to the author, care of the publisher (see copyright page for the postal address). Where possible, I will make an effort to include any suggestions for improved repair techniques received this way in subsequent editions of the book.

Finally, I would like to express my gratitude to the many people who have helped with this and earlier editions of the book. On the other hand, I do want to express my disappointment with the niggardly response from the U.S. distributors for the major component manufacturers. I really would have liked to be able to credit them for current information and illustrations about their products, but neither Shimano, nor SR SunTour, nor Campagnolo saw fit to even acknowledge my requests. I had to go to these companies' European offices to get help, for which I am deeply indebted to them.

Table of Contents

CHAPTER 1

Understanding Your Bicycle

The present book is intended to help you keep your bicycle in optimal condition. It will give you essentially all the information you ever need to keep the bike operating smoothly and efficiently, and to enable you to fix it when it does malfunction.

The approach of the book is simple: define the problem, identify the cause, and show what to do about it. I will go about it as systematically as possible, first explaining what can be the cause of a specific problem, then proceeding with a list of required tools — or ways to substitute for the right tools, if they can't be rounded up — and finally applying step-by-step instructions for alleviating the problem. Photographic illustrations and the occasional detail drawing allow you to identify parts and tools at a glance.

The emphasis is on the type of bicycles mostly sold these days, regular derailleur bikes and mountain bikes. However, this book also explains in detail the equipment that

Your bike seen head on.
Left: Typical modern road bike. Right: typical modern mountain bike.

is only found on other models, such as folding bikes, roadsters or even carrier bicycles. Thus, the three-speed hub, drum and roller-lever brakes, and even dynamo lighting equipment are covered by adequate instructions for their maintenance.

The Bicycle's Components

To do any work on the bike, it is necessary first to know just what we are talking about and what the various components of the machine are called. I shall now briefly describe its major components. Components will be treated separately as units, and together as groups. The following functional groups may be distinguished:
☐   The wheels
☐   The drivetrain
☐   The gearing system
☐   The brakes

The front end of a typical modern road bike with integrated brake and shift levers.

☐   The steering system
☐   The frame
☐   The saddle
☐   Accessories

Component Groups

Until recently, it was quite common to find a quality bicycle equipped with components from many different manufacturers. Brakes could be of one make, derailleurs of another, hubs of a third, the crankset might be supplied by yet another. Not so today, since what I call the "gruppo-craze" has set in, meaning that most parts are now sold together as a so-called *gruppo*, or component group-set. Due largely to extensive advertising and simultaneous commercial pressure from the two biggest component manufacturers (Shimano and Campagnolo), it has become fashionable to present the unitary look. Manufacturers are virtually forced to choose all their components from one supplier's various component groups, rather than selecting what they consider the most suitable individual makes and models, and the public has unjustly come to expect this.

Nice perhaps for the two big component makers, who indeed make just about everything, but unreasonably tough on those specialist suppliers who have invested all their efforts into particular components. Due to this recent craze, makers of superb brakes, hubs or crank-sets have run into serious problems, since the bicycle manufacturers who would like to install these products cannot get the other components individually: they either buy everything from Shimano or nothing. Even when obtaining parts from the same maker, they often have to be selected from one of many different gruppos.

This has sent some of the smaller manufacturers scrambling to also establish gruppos of their own. Thus, hub and derailleur maker SunTour teams up with brake manufacturer Dia-Compe and crankset maker SR to present its own gruppo with the name SunTour engraved on all parts. Similarly, some European manufacturers team up with others to present their own Mavic, Simplex, Modolo, Ofmega or Sachs sets, each containing selected items from other manufacturers.

The result is that the customer's and the manufacturer's choice is considerably narrowed down. What is even worse, the big manufacturers seem to be steering the bicycle industry away from one of its greatest virtues, namely the interchangeability of parts. Components are now no longer designed to be fully interchangeable with other makes

and models. Add to this the infuriating tendency not to stock spares of minor bits and pieces, and to change components from one year to the next, and you have arrived at a throw-away bicycle culture.

For the cyclist, this has made it more and more necessary to replace or repair parts by trial and error. No longer is it possible to predict with certainty whether a particular major or minor component will fit for replacement or repair. The moral is to always take the bike — or at least the matching components — to the shop when trying to obtain spares or replacement parts, to make sure things fit together before you buy.

Summary of Functional Groups

In the following paragraphs, I will briefly describe the various functional groups that make up the bicycle. This will serve as an overview of the bicycle and its components.

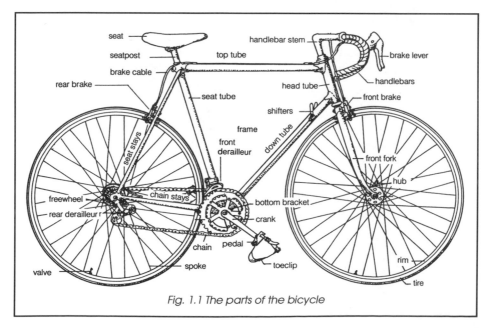

Fig. 1.1 The parts of the bicycle

The Wheels

The wheels, covered in Chapters 4 and 5, have flexible inner tubes and separate covers, except for true racing bikes, which have tubular tires, referred to sew-ups in the U.S., tubs in Britain. The tires are mounted on an aluminum rim that is held to the hub by means of spokes hooked into the central hub and screwed into nipples at the rim. The hub is held to the frame or the fork either with nuts threaded onto the axle or with a quick-release mechanism.

The Drivetrain

The drivetrain comprises the parts that transmit the rider's propulsive force or torque to the rear wheel. As described in Chapter 6, it consists of the crankset (called chain-set in Britain), the pedals, the chain, the chainrings and the freewheel block installed on the rear wheel hub.

The Gearing System

Nowadays, gearing generally means derailleurs, although hub gears still exist. A derailleur system is made up of the front and rear derailleurs, which move the chain from one combination of chainring and sprocket to another, and the shift levers mounted on the handlebars or the frame's downtube (depending on the kind of bike), as well as flexible cables that connect each shifter with its derailleur. Although quite rare in the U.S., hub gearing systems have gone through significant developments in recent years and can be expected to reappear on bikes intended for city use very soon. The maintenance of derailleurs and hub gearing systems are covered in Chapters 7 and 8, respectively.

The Brakes

The brakes are also (usually) controlled by means of flexible cables from levers mounted on the handlebars. Once you pull the brake lever, the brake itself stops the wheel by squeezing two brake pads against the side of the wheel rim. Special brakes built into the wheel hubs also exist. Brake maintenance will be covered in

Typical drivetrain of a modern bike with derailleur gearing.

Chapters 9 and 10 for rim brakes and hub brakes respectively.

The Steering System

The steering system, which is analyzed in Chapter 11, comprises the parts that allow balancing and steering the bike. These include the front fork, handlebars, stem, and headset bearings. This group allows the steering system to pivot relative to the rest of the bike when the handlebars are turned.

The Frame

The frame is covered in Chapter 12. It forms the backbone of the bicycle, on which the other components are installed. The frame is a series of tubes that have been welded or bonded together. They are the main frame (head tube, top tube, down tube and seat tube), as well as the pairs of thinner tubes that make up the rear triangle (seat stays and chain stays). In addition, there is a bottom bracket, at the point where down tube, seat tube and chain stays meet, and drop-outs which accept the rear axle. Fortunately, the frame rarely needs repair work. If it does get damaged, it's usually time to get a new bike.

The Saddle

The saddle is mounted to a seatpost, which in turn is clamped into the frame's seat tube. Its height and angle can be adjusted by means of the clamping devices that hold the seatpost to the frame and the saddle to the seatpost, respectively. This subject is described in Chapter 13.

Component gruppo: This one is made by Campagnolo. The major manufacturer is Shimano, but many other manufacturers also supply complete component groups like this one.

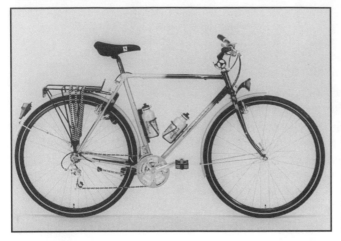

City bikes , like these, were developed in Europe and are making their way into the U.S. market. Essentially, they are mountain bikes with a wide range of accessories: luggage rack, fenders, chainguard, kick stand and lighting.

Accessories

Accessories are additional components that can be installed on the bicycle. The maintenance and/or installation of the saddle adjuster (Hite-Rite), lighting equipment, luggage racks (or carriers), fenders (or mudguards), and other small parts are covered in Chapter 14.

CHAPTER 2

Selecting Tools

This and the next chapter will be devoted to very general themes. First I'll survey the most important tools required to work on the bike. In Chapter 3 I'll proceed to explain such frequently encountered details as cable adjustment, threaded connections, quick-releases and ball bearings. That same chapter also gives some guidelines for general preventive maintenance, following a regular schedule.

Although it is possible to spend several thousand dollars on bicycle tools, at least 90% of all maintenance and repair work can be done with a very modest outfit. And of those tools, only a few are so essential that they should also be taken along on most bike trips on the road or the trail. These include universal tools that can be bought at any hardware shop, and specific bicycle tools that are available only from well-stocked bike shops or specialized mail order outlets.

Understanding Quality

Quality counts when buying tools even more than when dealing with most other products. I have found quite similar looking tools at prices that varied by a factor of three —and in my youthful ignorance I have only too often been seduced into buying the cheaper version. That's a mistake, because the tool that costs one-third as much doesn't last even a third as long. Besides, it never fits as accurately, often leading to damage both of the part handled and of the tool itself. After some unsatisfactory use, you'll probably decide to get the better tool anyway, so you end up spending quite a bit more than you would have done if you had bought the highest quality tool in the first place.

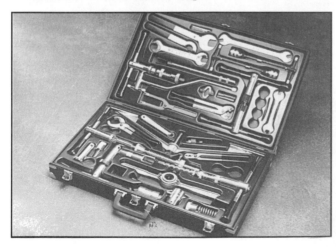

A selection of special bicycle-specific tools. Sets like these are available from major component makers, like Campagnolo, and tool manufacturers, such as VAR. For a lot less money, you can build up your own collection of essential tools, buying specific ones as you need them.

Having sworn to buy only the best tools for the job, we can now get down to a brief description of the various essential tools of both categories — universal tools and special bicycle tools. Even less common items, which are used only rarely if at all by the amateur bike mechanic, will be described in the chapters where their application becomes relevant.

Below, you will find most of the common tools described, some of them with an illustration. Don't be discouraged by the length of the list, since you don't really need every one of the items described here. Refer to the section on *Tools to Take Along* for the really essential tools that should be bought right away. All the other tools can wait until you have a specific need. Most bicycle components are now built with metric threading, and thus metric tool sizes will be required. The size quoted in mm (millimeters) will be the dimension across flats of the point where the tool fits — not the size of the screw thread, as is customary for American and Whitworth sizes.

The metric system is universally used for most bicycle components, and virtually all the tools will have metric size designations. If you're not familiar with the metric system, you may want to refer to the conversion table in the Appendix.

The specific tools to use for any one job are listed with the instructions in Chapters 4–14. However, your bike may not require each of those tools, so I recommend that you first check which are the ones needed for your bike.

Universal Tools

These are the basic tools that can be purchased in any hardware shop. I will point out which sizes are appropriate for mountain bike maintenance jobs.

Screwdriver

The screwdriver's size is designated by the blade width at the end. You will need a small one with a 4 mm (3/16 in.) blade, a larger one with a 6–7 mm (1/4–5/32 in.) blade, and perhaps a Phillips head model for screws with cross-shaped recesses instead of the conventional saw cut.

Adjustable wrench

These are designated by their overall length. Get a 150 mm (6 in.) long model and one that is at least 200 mm (8 in.), preferably even 250 mm (10 in.) long.

Box wrench

Called ring spanners in England, these are the most accurate tools for tightening or loosening nuts and bolts with hexagonal heads. Like all other fixed wrenches, they are designated by the across-flats dimension of the bolt on which they fit, always measured in mm. You will need sizes from 7 to 16 mm.

Open-ended wrench

These are the most common wrenches available. They can be used when there is not enough access room for the ring wrench. Get a set in sizes from 7 mm to 16 mm.

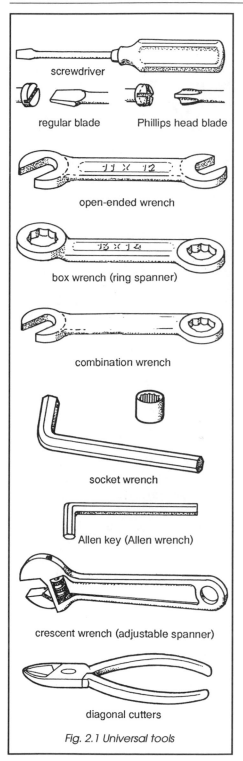

screwdriver

regular blade   Phillips head blade

open-ended wrench

box wrench (ring spanner)

combination wrench

socket wrench

Allen key (Allen wrench)

crescent wrench (adjustable spanner)

diagonal cutters

Fig. 2.1 Universal tools

Combination wrench

This type has a box wrench on one end and an open-ended wrench of the same size on the other. Even better than a set of each of the preceding items, is to get two sets of these (because for many jobs, you'll need two fixed wrenches of the same size), again in sizes from 7 mm to 16 mm.

Socket Wrench

These comprise a separate handle and interchangeable sockets that exactly fit around a particular size nut or bolt head on the one end, and a hexagonal recess to fit the handle on the other. Handles come in two sizes — 1/4 in. for the smaller sockets, and 3/8 in. for the larger sockets. Instead of the simple handle, you can use a torque wrench to limit the force applied, as will be discussed in Chapter 3.

Allen key

Also known as Allen wrench, these hexagonal L-shaped bars are used on the screws with hexagonal recesses often used on mountain bikes. They are designated by the across-flats dimension, and you will probably need these in sizes 2 mm to 9 mm. You can either get individual ones in selected sizes, or you can get a complete set. I find the latter quite handy, because individual ones tend to get lost or buried underneath other tools and parts.

Hammer

These are classified by their weight. I suggest a 300 gram (10 oz.) metalworking model, which square head at one end and wedge-shaped one at

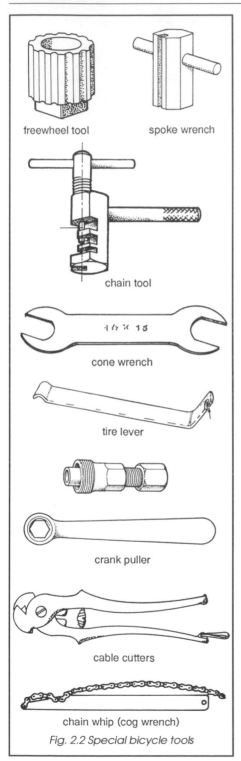

freewheel tool

spoke wrench

chain tool

cone wrench

tire lever

crank puller

cable cutters

chain whip (cog wrench)

Fig. 2.2 Special bicycle tools

the other. In addition, you may need a mallet with a plastic head of about the same weight.

Hacksaw

When all else fails, you may find a need for one of these, e.g. to remove a tangled or rusted part or to provide a hold for the screwdriver in a damaged bolt. They are designated by their blade length. I find the 8-in. Eclipse saw quite adequate.

Files

These are designated by the length of their blade and their coarseness. Get a relatively fine 8-inch-long model to file jagged outer cable ends or remove the occasional protruding spoke or a burr at the end of a part that is cut off or damaged.

Special Bicycle Tools

The following list of tools made specifically for bicycle use includes almost all the tools you will be likely to need as a home mechanic. A much more modest selection — those listed under *Tools to Take Along* — will usually get you by when no really major operations have to be carried out.

Even more specialized tools will be mentioned as we get into the actual maintenance instructions. In many cases, you will have to consult the bike shop to make sure you get the size or model of any particular tool that matches the parts installed on your bike. For that reason, it is best to have the bike with you whenever buying tools.

Pump

Although often considered an accessory rather than a tool, it's also an essential tool, especially on the mountain bike, since you may be riding the bike far from the nearest gas station or garage. Make sure you get a model that matches the particular valves used on your bike (Presta or Schrader, as described in Chapter 5). Increasingly frame-fit pumps are now equipped with both Presta and Schrader fittings, especially if they are intended for mountain bike use. A CO_2 inflator will speed up the process, but each full tire inflation may require a new cartridge, so it's not much use except when you are racing.

Pressure gauge

In addition to the pump, I suggest you invest in a pressure gauge to make sure you inflate the tires correctly, at least to use at home — again matching the valve on your bicycle's tires, or buy an adaptor to convert it to the appropriate valve type.

Tire levers

These are now usually made of plastic. They are used to lift the tire off the rim in case of a puncture or when replacing tube or tire. Select thin, flat ones that don't bend. Most mountain bike tires fit loosely enough on the rim to need only one or two, and some can actually be removed without.

Tire repair kit

The tire repair kit contains most of the other essentials for fixing a puncture, such as patches, rubber solution, and sandpaper. This little box also comes in handy to carry other small spare parts, such as duct tape for emergency repairs, extra nuts and bolts, pump washers, and light bulbs.

Spoke wrench

Also referred to as a spoke key or nipple spanner, it is used to tighten, remove or install a spoke. Quality is especially important when purchasing these — get the individual color-coded spoke wrench that fits your spokes.

A complete selection of special bicycle lubricants.

Crank bolt wrench

This tool is usually sold together with the crank extractor described below. The wrench part is needed to tighten or loosen the crank attachment bolts. Make sure you get one that matches the cranks installed on your bike, since they vary from make to make, sometimes even from model to model.

Crank extractor

This part threads into the crank center, and pulls it off the bottom bracket spindle. Once again, quality counts, so buy a good one — in the size to match the make and model of your cranks.

Freewheel tool

Used to remove a freewheel block from the rear hub. This tool must be selected to match the particular freewheel used on your bike.

Chain whip (cog wrench)

This device is used to remove individual sprockets from the freewheel. Depending on the kind of freewheel on your bike, you may either need two, or one used in conjunction with the manufacturer's special wrench.

Chain rivet extractor

Also known simply as chain tool, this one is used to thrust out a pin in any link of the chain so it can be separated for maintenance.

Cone wrench

These very flat open-ended wrenches are used to overhaul the bearings of a wheel hub. Available in several sizes — get two of each of the sizes needed for the hubs on your bike.

Bottom bracket tools

Needed for maintenance operation on the bottom bracket bearings. Many bikes are equipped with bottom brackets that need quite specific tools for this work, so make sure to match the tools to the components on your bike.

Headset tools

These are oversize, flat open-ended wrenches used to overhaul the steering system's headset bearings. Since the introduction of oversize (OS) headsets, their sizes and shapes also vary.

Lubricants and Cleaning Aids

In addition to the tools listed above, you will need some materials to help you clean the bike and its parts and to lubricate for minimum friction and maximum durability. Use the following items:

Bearing grease

Either the special kind sold under the brand name of bicycle component manufacturers, such as Phil Wood or Campagnolo, or any regular lithium-based bearing grease.

Oil

You can use special bicycle lubricants such as Finish Line, Pedros, or any mineral oil ranging from SAE 40 motor oil to SAE 60 gear oil.

Chain lube

Any bicycle chain lubricant will do. Pedros and Finish Line are two good ones that I have used.

Penetrating oil

A spraycan of thin, highly penetrating solvent-based lubricant, such as WD-40 or the lightest grade of LPS to loosen things such as rusty nuts and bolts, which will come loose after they are soaked for a few minutes.

Anti-Seize Lubricant

This is a paste-like compound that should be applied to screw-threaded connections between steel and aluminum parts to prevent binding.

Solvents

Preferable to paraffin oil, there are environmentally safe citrus oil-based solvents, such as those made by Finish Line, available from many bike shops. Do not use paint thinner, since that will dissolve not only dirt and grease, but also paint and even the cement used for bonded frames and components.

Wax

Bare metal surfaces as well as painted ones are best protected with car wax, applied after cleaning. Don't use regular furniture wax, since that often contains solvents that might attack the painted or aluminum surfaces.

Containers

A flat container to catch drips while lubricating or cleaning, and a jar to clean out small parts and brushes.

Cloths

You'll need at least one clean and one greasy rag. The latter is made that way by applying bearing grease or

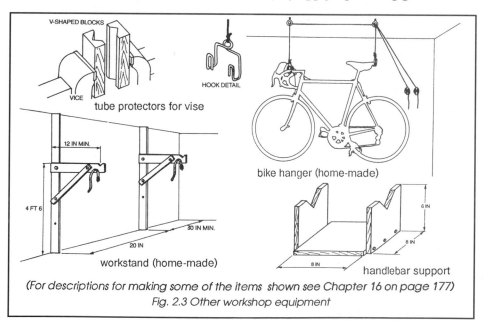

tube protectors for vise

bike hanger (home-made)

workstand (home-made)

handlebar support

(For descriptions for making some of the items shown see Chapter 16 on page 177)
Fig. 2.3 Other workshop equipment

oil — or simply after you've used it as a clean rag for some time.

Brushes

Get two sizes of regular paint brushes, about 2 and 4 cm (¾ and 1½ in.) wide, respectively. For cleaning in tight places, the most suitable brushes are the cylindrical bottle brushes, which are also available in several sizes.

Other cleaning aids

Many cleaning jobs are done simply with a rag and water, while some may require the use of a mixture of paraffin oil or another solvent with about 5–10% mineral oil.

Tools to Take Along

Only a very limited selection of the tools listed above are so essential that you should carry them along on your rides. On the mountain bike, or whenever your trip takes you far away from bike shops and service stations, you should probably be more generous in what to take along than you might be when riding on paved roads in built-up areas, since there is not much chance of getting help on the way, let alone hitching a ride home. The following lists just my personal preference — feel free to expand this list to suit your own needs.

After you have had some experience, you may decide to expand or modify this list to include the items you are most comfortable with. Whatever you select, perhaps the most important thing to keep in mind is to check the sizes and the types of tools that are needed for the jobs on your bike. There is no point carrying tools for equipment that is not in-

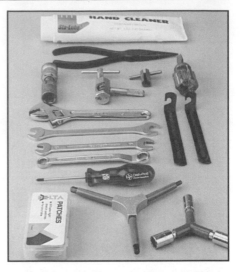

This is one cyclist's choice of essential tools to take along.

stalled on your particular bike. On the other hand, if you are traveling with a group, you may decide to carry just one tool kit with the appropriate equipment for all the bikes. This makes sense on a longer tour, where every ounce you carry counts and there is adequate preparation time.

Carry them in a bag tied to the bike, or make a pouch as illustrated, carried either in a bike bag or tied directly to a frame tube or under the saddle. Select a bag that does not dangle freely; it should be strapped to the seat pillar and the saddle. Here's what I suggest taking along:

- ☐ pump
- ☐ 2 or 3 tire levers
- ☐ tire patch kit
- ☐ 4 mm screwdriver
- ☐ 6-inch crescent wrench
- ☐ 2, 3, 4, 5, 6 mm Allen keys
- ☐ needle-nose pliers
- ☐ spoke wrench
- ☐ chain rivet tool
- ☐ crank bolt wrench

CHAPTER 3

Working on the Bike

The first part of this chapter will be devoted to the techniques for handling some basic mechanisms found in many places on any bicycle. This includes screw-threaded connections in general, various kinds of cables and their adjustment, ball bearings and their adjustment and lubrication, as well as the use of quick-releases, and wedge connections. The second part of this chapter will be devoted to preventive maintenance.

Screw Thread

Many of the bicycle's parts are attached, installed and themselves constructed with threaded connections — not only nuts and bolts, but many other components as well. Essentially all threaded connections are based on the same principle: a cylindrical (male) part is threaded into a corresponding hollow (female) part by means of matching helical grooves cut into each. When the male part is threaded fully into the female, the reaction force pushes the sides of the male and female threads against one another, creating so much friction that the parts are no longer free to turn, thus keeping the connection firm.

The best way to work on your bike is with some kind of bicycle workstand. Left: full size workstand from Blackburn Right: simple display stand.

Screw threads are designated by their nominal size, generally measured in millimeters in the bicycle industry. In addition, the pitch, or number of threads per inch, and the thread angle may vary, and finally some parts have left-hand (LH) threading, instead of the usual right-hand (RH) thread. Whereas most connections use RH threading, LH thread is found on the left pedal, as well as on a few bearing parts in the drivetrain, including bottom brackets.

Most nuts and bolts are standardized — for a given nominal diameter, they will have the same pitch and the same thread angle, and they all have RH thread. Many other bicycle components are less standardized There are at least three different industry standards for such parts as head-sets, bottom brackets and freewheels. Though virtually all British-built bikes — in fact most bikes sold in Britain, wherever they are made — are built to the BCI (British Cycle Institute) standard dimensions, chances are you will buy a component some day that turns out to have either French or Italian threading. To avoid such mismatching, always take the part to be replaced, as well as a matching component to which it is threaded, to the bike shop when buying a replacement, so you can try it out there.

Whether we are talking about an ordinary nut-and-bolt or any other threaded part, the way to loosen and tighten the connection is the same. The one part has to be restrained, while the other is turned relative to it. You turn it to the right to tighten, the left to loosen. ("Rightie tightie, leftie loosie" is a popular bike shop mnemonic.) Use accurately fitting tools to give the best possible hold and to minimize damage. Use tools with adequate leverage (e.g. a wrench with a long handle) on the part that is turned, while the part that is merely restrained may be held with less leverage (a screwdriver or a shorter wrench).

All threaded connections should be clean and lightly greased when they are installed. If you have difficulty loosening a connection, first squirt some penetrating oil, such as WD-40, at any accessible point where the male part disappears into the female part. To allow a nut or the head of a bolt to be turned when it is tightly fastened to the part it holds, a plain washer should be installed between the two. This allows you to tighten the joint more firmly and eases dismantling as well. To prevent binding of threaded connections between steel and aluminum parts, apply some special anti-seize lubricant to the screw threads before assembly.

To minimize the chances of coming loose because of vibrations caused while riding, many threaded connections are further secured by one means or another. These are the locknut, spring washer and locking-insert nut. The locknut is a second nut that is tightened against the main nut, creating high friction forces in the threads working in opposite ways. The spring washer expands to hold the connection when vibration would otherwise loosen it, and the locking insert nut has a nylon insert that is deformed by the threading, offering the required high resistance against loosening. If you have problems with parts coming loose, you may use any of these techniques to secure them. A connection that comes loose frequently despite the use of a locking device is probably worn to the point where replacement — usually of both parts — is in order.

Nuts, bolts and screws come in several versions, each requiring specific tools. Conventional nuts and bolts have hexagonal heads and are tightened, loosened or held with either an open-ended wrench, a socket wrench, or a ring wrench (preferably the latter, because it fits more accurately, with less chance of damage). Screws can have a regular straight saw cut, for use of a conventional screwdriver, or a cross-shaped, or Phillips head, for use with a Phillips screwdriver. In recent years, more and more bicycle parts are held with Allen bolts, which have a hexagonal recess for use of an Allen key. As long as tools of exactly matching sizes are used — in preference to oversized and adjustable ones), and

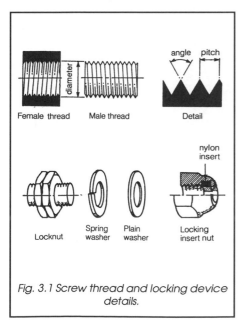

Fig. 3.1 Screw thread and locking device details.

you don't apply excessive force, you should be able to tighten every connection adequately without doing damage. If you notice excessive resistance, it will be better to replace the threaded parts than to use oversize tools or brute force.

Locking Threaded Connections

However firmly attached to begin with, many threaded connections come apart after cycling due to vibration. This applies most notably to parts that are attached in only one place, since this causes an imbalance aggravated by vibration. For this reason, care must be taken to attach accessories in two or more locations whenever possible, and to frequently retighten single attachments — or use at least two mounting points.

In order to minimize the effect of vibrations, several locking devices have been developed, some of which are shown in Fig. 3.1: locknut, locking insert nut, spring washer and lock washer. The latter is shaped to match a longitudinal groove cut in the male part to accept the inward pointing key on the washer.

Another solution, that cannot be shown in any illustration, is the use of a thread locking compound, such as Locktite. This compound is available in at least two versions with different bonding strengths — use the one in the blue bottle to secure threaded connections that you will need to take apart again.

Although all the solutions mentioned above work to some extent, even these have to be checked and retightened regularly. In the case of the locknut, the inner nut must first be tightened independently, after which the outer nut is tightened against the inner nut.

Torque and Leverage

When tightening or loosening screw threaded connections, accurately fitting tools with correct leverage must be used to provide the right torque. Excessive torque can damage parts, while too little torque leads to inadequately tightened connections (or, when trying to loosen a connection, would not suffice to do so). Some manufacturers specify the torque that should be used, which can be controlled by means of special torque wrenches. For the home mechanic, it will generally be sufficient to make sure tools of the right size are used.

Torque is a measure of the force applied to a screw threaded connection when tightening or loosening it. It is a function of the length of the tool's leverage and the force applied by hand to the end. In practice, overtightening can be as harmful as undertightening. The size and the material of the connection determine how much torque can be applied safely.

The best way to avoid damage is by using a special tool called a torque wrench — it can be set to the limiting torque value for the specific connection. This is of course the sophisticated approach and for those who want to take things that seriously, I have provided recommended torque values for a number of critical connections in the Appendix.

Even if you don't want to invest in a torque wrench and a complete set of matching bits for each type of application (screws, hexagon bolts, and Allen bolts), you should still be aware of the concept. As long as you

make sure threaded parts are clean and intact, you use a tool of the correct size, and you use less force for fittings in plastic and aluminum than for those in plastic, you will probably be able to operate safely. If you do damage a threaded connection, take it to the bike shop and get matching replacement parts rather than fudging things.

Matching Tools to the Job

Screwdrivers must match the size of the saw cuts or the size of the cross-shaped recess in Phillips-head screws. Allen keys of the exactly matching size must be used on bolts with hexagonal recesses. Use open-ended wrenches or (preferably) box wrenches that exactly fit on hexagonal nuts and bolts. When using two tools that do not have the same leverage (measured as their handle length perpendicular to the axis of the connection) use the tool with the longer lever on the part to be moved, the shorter one on the stationary part.

Wrenches are supplied with increasing handle size as their nominal sizes go up to provide correct leverage. Fastened by hand, with the correct size wrench perpendicular to the axis of the connection, the chance of damaging the connection by overtightening is minimal. When using an adjustable wrench, select a short one for small nuts, a larger one for larger ones to prevent excessive torque. To loosen a particularly stubborn connection, apply penetrating oil, such as WD-40 to the threads before resorting to tricks to increase leverage (e.g. by means of a length of steel tubing around the handle of a wrench).

Buying Replacements and Tools

Whenever you have to buy a replacement part for the bike, it is best to take either the whole bike or at least the old part and one matching component (e.g. the nut as well as the bolt, the handlebars as well as the stem, when replacing either one) to the shop with you to make sure you get perfectly matching components.

The same goes for buying tools for specific jobs, because many makes and models of similar parts exist that may vary in size, each requiring its own matching tool.

Control Cables

Brakes and gears on the bicycle are operated via so-called Bowden cables, consisting of an inner cable and an outer casing. The inner cable transmits tension forces, which are countered by the compression forces taken up by the outer cable, or casing.

The inner cable has a nipple at one end, while the other end is clamped at the brake or gear mechanism. Ferrules are installed at the ends of the outer cable to provide a firm termination at the anchor

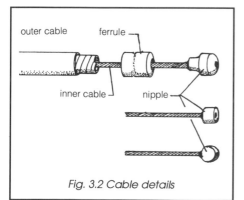

Fig. 3.2 Cable details

points. A new crimp should always be clamped around the free end of the inner cable to prevent fraying, or it can be soldered. There will be several different cables on your bike, and you should take care to get the right kind. In addition to the different nipple shapes in use by different makers to match particular components, the thickness can vary.

The inner cables for index gearing controls are designed to be rather stiff so they can take up some compressive, as well as tensile, forces. The inner cables for brake controls must be quite thick to take up the high forces without stretching. Make sure the diameters of inner and outer cables are matched correctly so the inner cable can slide through freely.

The cables for the brakes and those for conventional (non-indexed) derailleurs should be cleaned and lubricated regularly, while the ones for indexed derailleurs should only be kept clean, without lubrication. The index system invariably uses a stainless steel inner cable with a nylon sleeve between it and the inside of the casing, which makes lubrication unnecessary.

By way of lubrication for a regular cable, you may put some grease on a rag and run this rag over the inner cable. Once the cable is installed, you may use spraycan lubricant, aiming with the nozzle at the points where the inner cable disappears into the casing. Remove excess lubricant with a rag to keep things clean.

When replacing cables, I suggest using stainless steel inner cables. Whether stainless or not, make sure you select them with a nipple of the same shape and size used on the original, matching the recess of the relevant lever. Some cable casings are available with a low-friction liner of either nylon or PTFE (usually referred to as teflon); these eliminate a lot of potential maintenance problems.

Adjusting the cable tension is often necessary to adjust brakes or gears. Before attempting adjustment, make sure the cable end is clamped in firmly. To adjust, loosen the lock nut (usually a round knurled design), while restraining the adjusting barrel. Next, unscrew the adjusting barrel far enough to obtain the desired cable tension, and finally tighten the locknut while holding the adjusting barrel to restrain it.

If the length of the adjusting barrel does not allow enough adjusting range, the clamping point on the other end of the inner cable must be moved. To do this, first back up the adjuster locknut all the way while restraining the adjusting barrel, then screw the adjusting barrel in all the way, and finally clamp the cable in a new position, while keeping it pulled taut with the aid of a pair of pliers.

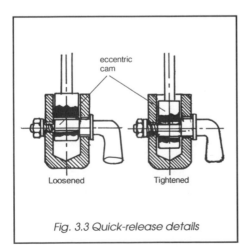

Fig. 3.3 Quick-release details

Push-Pull Cables

For some applications, a different version of the Bowden cable has been used, mainly for a few special derailleur and hub gear controls. On this type, the inner cable itself consists of two layers, the first one of which is conventional, while the outer layer is rolled from a flat band. This allows the inner cable to take both tension (pull) and compression (push) forces. These cables are extremely tough to cut—even if you do have the appropriate tool. Consequently, they are best bought made-to-measure, complete with the matching outer casing.

Quick-Releases

Quick-release (QR) mechanisms are used on the hubs of many bikes, and on the seat clamp of the mountain bike, while many brakes or their levers also come equipped with some mechanism to de-tension the brake cable quickly. The quick-releases for the saddle clamp and wheel hubs work on the same principle. Instead of holding the axle or bolt by means of one or two nuts that are screwed down, a toggle lever is used.

The thumb nut at the other end is not to be used to tighten the connection, but merely to adjust it in such a way that twisting the lever tightens the whole connection firmly. Open the lever by twisting it, close it by twisting it back. If the connection does not hold, first place the lever in the open position, then tighten the thumbnut perhaps half a turn and try again, until the lever not only holds the part firmly, but can also be opened enough to allow removal or adjustment.

Recently, specialized wheel and seat clamp QR mechanisms have been introduced by some manufacturers that require a special maneuver to open and close in order to prevent unintentional loosening. Other manufacturers place a retention device between the fork-end and the quick-release to prevent unintentional loosening. These devices must be flipped out of the way to release or install the wheel.

Ball Bearings

There are at least 14 ball bearing units in every bicycle. They are two each in the hubs, the head-set, the pedals, the bottom bracket and the freewheel. They all work on the same principle and their condition has a great effect on the bike's performance. Understanding their operation, maintenance and adjustment is as important for every home bike mechanic as it is for the occasional cyclist who just wants to be sure his bike is operating optimally.

Two kinds of ball bearings are in use, the cup-and-cone, or adjustable type, and cartridge bearings (often referred to as sealed bearings). In either case, *ball bearing* does not mean one of the little balls used, but the whole assembly, while the little balls are correctly called *bearing balls*.

Although cartridge bearings are generally more accurate when new, and can be better sealed against dirt and water, they are not inherently superior. Besides, there is little maintenance you can do on these models. Either they run smoothly or they must be replaced, which generally requires special tools. Sometimes — but not usually — lubrication is allowed for by means of an oil hole or a grease nipple in the part in which the bearings are installed. In other cases, the best you can do is to lift off the seal with a pointed tool and apply grease.

The more common cup-and-cone bearing consists of a cone-shaped and a cup-shaped bearing race, one of which is adjustable relative to the other by means of screw threading. The bearing balls lie in the recess between these two parts and are lubricated to minimize friction. Generally, bearing grease is used as a lubricant.

Normal grease lubrication only has to be repacked once a year. But to do it, you have to dismantle the entire bearing, as explained in the relevant chapters. Clean and inspect all parts, replacing anything that appears to be damaged (corroded, pitted or grooved). Then fill the cup-shaped bearing race with bearing grease and push the new bearing balls in, leaving enough space to allow their free movement, followed by reassembly and subsequent adjustment.

Some bearings are equipped with a system of seals and grease nipples

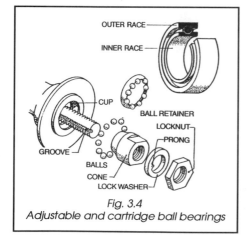

OUTER RACE
INNER RACE
CUP
BALL RETAINER
LOCKNUT
PRONG
GROOVE
BALLS
CONE
LOCK WASHER

Fig. 3.4
Adjustable and cartridge ball bearings

that allow the injection of grease without it filling the entire area inside the component. These are referred to as Grease Guard and they are lubricated by injecting grease with a matching grease gun available from the same manufacturer. This method is especially suitable for mountain bike components and for bikes often ridden in wet or dusty terrain, for which repacking with grease just once a year would be inadequate.

Adjustable bearings must be so adjusted that the moving part is free to rotate with minimal friction, yet has no play or looseness. To adjust a cup-and-cone bearing, loosen the locknut or lockring while holding the underlying cone (in the case of a hub or a pedal), or the cup (in the case of a headset or bottom bracket). Next, lift the underlying lock washer, if installed, and tighten or loosen the threaded main bearing cone or cup about a quarter of a turn at a time. Finally hold that part again, while tightening the locknut or lockring. Repeat the whole operation if necessary.

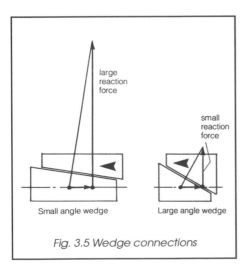

Fig. 3.5 Wedge connections

Wedge Connections

This method of attachment is used in various locations on the bicycle by means of matching tapered or conically shaped surfaces. Typical applications of this method are found in the attachment of the cranks to the bottom bracket spindle and the handlebar stem to the front fork.

The principle of the wedge connection is that a given axially applied force transfers a much increased lateral or radial force when applied via a slanted surface, proportional to the slope. The maximum connecting force is thus achieved by choosing the angle of the wedge surface relative to the axis as small as practicable.

Since, on the other hand, the relative displacement increases inversely proportional to the slope, the parts must be made more accurately matching and of less deforming materials as the angle is made smaller. This applies especially to the connection between cranks and bottom bracket spindle, while the situation is much less critical in the case of the handlebar stem attachment.

When wedge connections come loose, it is mainly because the deformation of one part relative to the other increases the play, thus reducing the contact pressure. This applies mainly to cheaper components, made of relatively soft materials and short contact surfaces.

Any wedge connection, especially when new, must be tightened frequently — once a week or before every long ride during the first month. This prevents damage done by a loosening connection and keeps the connection trouble-free without need for frequent tightening from then on. Another important precaution is to clean and slightly lubricate the contact surfaces, which prevents seizing.

Workshop and Bike Support

When you are out in terrain or on the road, you can't be too picky, but when doing maintenance or repair work at home, I recommend you provide an organized workshop space. It needn't be a separate room or a permanently designated location. But while working on the bike, it should be adequately equipped for doing so.

The amount of space needed is quite modest: 2.10 × 1.80 m (7 ft. × 6 ft.) is enough for any maintenance work ever done on the bike. As a minimum, you should equip this area with the tools and the cleaning and lubrication aids listed in the preceding chapter. In addition, you will need a workbench — although the kitchen counter or an old table will do. Ideally, you should install a sizable metalworking vice on the workbench, although probably 98% of all the jobs described in this book can be carried out without it.

Next, you will want a support for the bike. The best ones are freestanding devices or those mounted against the wall. I suggest you buy a bike stand that will support the bike off the ground. A simpler but adequate solution is to turn the bike upside down, supporting it at the handlebars by means of a home-made device. It serves to raise the handlebars off the ground far enough to protect anything mounted there.

Mountain bikes and other models with flat handlebars can usually be placed upside down

without such a support, merely turning the shifters out of the way to protect them, and that is what you will have to do when you have a problem while far from home. Just don't forget to do that each time you turn it over without adequate support, using a 5 mm Allen key to loosen the clamps that attach the shifters — and tightening them again in the proper positions when you have finished.

Preventive Maintenance

At the risk of being trite, I must emphasize that in bicycle maintenance, an ounce of prevention is worth a pound of repairs. It is actually very simple to keep the bike in good operating condition, so it is working well whenever you ride it. That will eliminate the vast majority of unanticipated repairs later on. It's all a matter of knowing what to look for and how to put it right before it becomes serious. It will be easy enough to spot when a nut or a bearing has come loose, and if corrected immediately, no harm will be done. Yet left unchecked, the situation rapidly becomes worse, often leading to an expensive and complicated replacement job after only a week or so of neglect.

Although most of the actual maintenance operations are covered in detail in the chapters that follow, this is the time to get familiar with a systematic schedule to check the bike. It is based on (almost) daily, monthly and annual checks, proceeding as outlined below. These are merely lists of jobs that need to be done; for the actual instructions telling you exactly how to go about it, and what to do to correct any problems you encounter, refer to the individual chapters that follow, each of which deals with a particular system or group of components on the bike.

Daily Inspection

This may seem to be overdoing it a little, but there are a few things you ought to look out for whenever you take the bike out. These will be covered in this section.

Quick-Release Mechanisms:
Check quick-release mechanisms on wheels. If they can't be tightened, first put the lever in the *open* position, then tighten the thumb nut one or two turns, and the lever into the *closed* position

Tires:
Check whether the tires are inflated properly, considering the type of terrain you will ride in: 6–7 bar (90–105 psi) for a racing bike on smooth roads, 4–5 bar (60–75 psi) for touring bikes, mountain bikes and hybrids on smooth, hard roads, 3 bar (45 psi) for mountain bikes on rough but hard surfaces, 2 bar (30 psi) for mountain bikes on loose and irregular surfaces.

Handlebars:
Make sure the handlebars are straight, at the right height, and cannot be easily twisted from side to side.

Saddle:
Verify that it is straight, level, securely attached to the seat post and at the right height.

Brakes:
Check the effectiveness of the brakes by verifying each can block the wheel against your weight pushing the bike forward with the lever depressed, leaving about 2 cm (¾ in.) between brake lever and handlebars.

Gears:
Lift the rear wheel and, while turning the cranks, check whether the derailleurs can be shifted to reach every combination of chainring and sprocket. However, avoid combining the largest chainring with the largest sprocket, or the smallest chainring with the smallest sprocket.

Monthly Inspection

At least once a month during the time you use the bike, clean it as explained below. Then carry out the same inspections listed above for the daily inspection, and in addition do the following:

Wheels:
Check for broken spokes and wheel wobble. Lift the wheel off the ground and turn it relatively slowly, keeping an eye on a fixed point such as the brake blocks. If the wheel seems to wobble sideways relative to the fixed point, it should be trued.

Brakes:
Observe what happens when you pull the brake levers forcefully. The brake blocks must touch the side of the rim over their entire surface when the lever is pulled hard. Adjust the brake as outlined in Chapter 9 if they don't.

Tires:
Check the tires for external damage and embedded objects. Remove anything that doesn't belong there and replace the tire if necessary.

Cranks:
Using the crank extractor tool, tighten the crank attachment nuts or bolts, as explained in Chapter 6.

General inspection:
Check all the other bolts and nuts to make sure they are tight, verify whether all moving parts turn freely and all adjustments are correct. Repair or replace anything damaged or missing.

Lubrication:
Lubricate the small moving parts, using the lubricants indicated below and wiping any excess off afterwards.

☐ **Chain:** Use special chain lube.
☐ **Exposed uncoated metal parts:** Use bicycle polish or car wax.
☐ **Brake levers, pivots, cables:** Spray a light lubricant, aiming precisely with the little tubular nozzle installed on the spray head.

Annual Inspection:

The work described below will be necessary at least once a year, twice a year if you ride a lot in bad weather both summer and winter. This is a complete overhauling job, which very nearly returns the bike to its as-bought condition. Treated this way, your bike will last a lifetime.

If you only use the bike in the fair-weather period, carry out this work at the end of the season. Then merely carry out a monthly inspec-tion at the beginning of the next season. During the annual inspection, proceed as follows:

First carry out all the work described above for the monthly inspection, noting in particular which parts need special attention because they seem to be loose, worn, damaged or missing. Subsequently, work down the following list.

Wheels:
With the wheels still in the bike, check for damage of the rim, the tire and missing spokes, then take the wheel out and overhaul the hubs, as described in Chapter 4, repacking them with bearing grease. This work is not necessary if the hubs have cartridge bearings, as long as they are operating perfectly smoothly and without play. It is a good idea to put a drop of light oil, such as 3-in-One, under the cartridge bearing seal.

Hubs:
Check the hubs for play, wear and tightness as explained in Chapter 4. Preferably, dismantle and lubricate or overhaul the hubs.

Chain:
Remove the chain and measure the length of a 100-link section (i.e. the distance between the first and the fiftieth pin). Replace the entire chain if it measures more than 51 in. (129.5 cm). The apparent stretch is a sign of wear that will affect shifting and transmission efficiency. In addition, the worn chain will also wear out the chainrings and the sprockets. If you replace the chain, you may have to replace one or more sprockets as well. If the chain is not badly worn, merely rinse it out in solvent, after

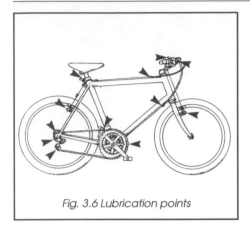

Fig. 3.6 Lubrication points

Cleaning the Bike

Do this job whenever your bike gets dirty — at least once a month in clean terrain and dry weather, much more frequently in bad weather or muddy terrain.

Cleaning procedure:

1. If the bike is dry, wipe it with a soft brush or a rag to remove any dust and other dry dirt. If the bike — or the dirt that adheres to it — is wet, hose or sponge it down with plenty of clean water. Take care not to get the water into the hubs, bottom bracket and head-set bearings, though. The same goes for a leather saddle.

which it should be lubricated and reinstalled, following the instructions in Chapter 6.

Bottom bracket:
Check it for play and freedom of rotation. If the bottom bracket is of the adjustable type, remove the crank and dismantle and overhaul the bearings as explained in Chapter 6. If it has cartridge bearings and does not spin properly, get it replaced at the bike shop or replace it yourself.

2. Using a damp rag or toothbrush, clean in all the hard-to-reach nooks and crannies. Make sure you get into all the hidden places, like between the sprockets on the freewheel and chainrings, underneath the brake arms, or at the derailleur pulleys.

Headset:
Try it out and make sure it rotates without play or rough spots. Preferably, disassemble and overhaul the bearings as described in Chapter 11.

3. Clean and dry the same areas with a clean, soft, dry rag.

4. With a clean wax- or grease-soaked rag, treat all the bare metal areas very sparingly to inhibit rust.

Derailleurs:
With the chain removed, clean, check and lubricate both derailleur mechanisms, making sure the pivots work smoothly and the little wheels (or pulleys) of the rear derailleur turn freely. On mountain bikes, the upper pulley is often worn, owing to dirt and debris; so it must be replaced. If necessary, overhaul or replace parts as explained in Chapter 7.

5. Twice a year, it may be worthwhile to apply car wax to the paintwork. At the same time, any chrome-plated and bare metal parts may be treated with chrome polish, followed by an application of wax.

CHAPTER 4

The Wheels

The bicycle wheel consists of hub, rim, tire, tube, and spokes. One end of the spokes is hooked onto the hub flange, and the other end is connected with the rim by means of a screwed-on nipple. This chapter will be devoted to the wheel itself, while tire-related work is treated separately in Chapter 5.

Wheel problems are the primary cause of bicycle breakdowns, especially if you ride off-road frequently. In this chapter we shall cover all the major maintenance and repair operations required.

First you will be shown how to replace the wheel most effectively, as is often necessary to transport the bike or to carry out other maintenance jobs.

Replace Wheel with Quick-Release

Quick-release hubs are now used extensively on road bikes and mountain bikes alike.

Tools and equipment:
• rag (for rear wheel)

Removal procedure:

1. If you are working on the rear wheel, first put the chain on the smallest sprocket and the smallest chainring by means of the derailleur, while turning the cranks with the wheel raised off the ground.

2. If your tire is flat, it will easily pass through the brake pads.

3. To allow an inflated tire to pass between the brake pads, release the

brake. On road bikes that is done by flipping the brake quick release. On mountain bikes it is done by squeezing the brake arms against the rim and unhooking the straddle cable QR nipple (on cantilever brake or U-brake) or by twisting the cam plate out (on the roller-cam brake). In the case of an under-the-chainstay U-brake, just push the wheel forward in the drop-outs until it hits the inside of the brake, spreading the brake arms apart.

4. Twist the hub's quick-release lever to the *open* position.

5. On the rear wheel, pull back the derailleur and the chain, using a rag to keep your hands clean. Pull out the wheel, guiding it past the brake pads.

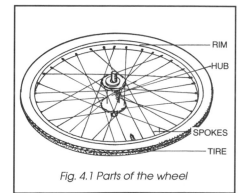

Fig. 4.1 Parts of the wheel

RIM
HUB
SPOKES
TIRE

Installation procedure:

1. If you are working on the rear wheel, first put the shifters in the position to engage the gear with the chain on the smallest sprocket and the smallest chainring. Turn the cranks forward if you have to engage another chainring in the front.

2. To allow the tire to pass between the brake shoes, make sure the the brake is released — if not, squeeze the brake arms together and un-hook one of the QR nipples (on can-tilever brake or U-brake) or twist the cam plate out (on the roller-cam brake).

3. Twist the lever on the hub's quick-release to the open position.

4. On the rear wheel, pull back the derailleur and the chain.

5. Slide the wheel back into position, guiding it past the brake pads.

6. Straighten the wheel exactly be-tween fork blades or chain stays and seat stays.

7. Holding the wheel in the correct position, flip the quick-release lever to the *closed* position and make sure the wheel is locked firmly in place.

8. Verify you have installed the wheel perfectly centered.

9. Tension the brake or reinstall the QR nipple, then readjust the brake.

Replace Wheel with Axle Nuts

Still used on many roadsters and other low-end bikes, the attachment by means of axle nuts is in no way in-ferior. Here's how to go about remov-ing and installing such a wheel.

Tools and equipment:
- 13 or 15 mm wrench
- rag

Removal procedure

1. If you are working on the rear wheel, first put the chain on the

Installation of wheel without quick-release, showing a retainer hooked into the fork-end

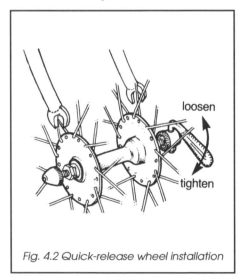

Fig. 4.2 Quick-release wheel installation

smallest sprocket and the smallest chainring by means of the derailleur, while turning the cranks with the rear wheel raised off the ground.

2. To allow the tire to pass between the brake pads, release the brake by squeezing the brake arms against the rim and unhook one of the QR nipples (on cantilever brake or U-brake) or twist the cam plate out (on the roller-cam brake). On a mountain bike with under-the-chainstay U-brake, push the wheel forward against the inside of the brake to spread the brake arms apart.

3. Loosen both axle nuts by two or three turns.

4. On the rear wheel, pull back the derailleur and the chain.

5. Pull out the wheel, guiding it past the brake pads.

Installation procedure:

1. If you are working on the rear wheel, first put the shifters in the position to engage the gear with the chain on the smallest sprocket and the smallest chainring. Turn the cranks forward if you have to engage another chainring in the front.

2. To allow the tire to pass between the brake shoes, make sure the the brake is released — if not, open the quick-release (on road bike brakes) or squeeze the brake arms together and unhook the straddle cable's QR nipples (on cantilever brake or U-brake) or twist the cam plate out (on the roller-cam brake).

3. Install the washers (if the axle nuts do not have integral washers) between the drop-outs and the nuts.

4. On the rear wheel, pull back the derailleur and the chain.

5. Slide the wheel back into position, guiding it past the brake pads, and center the rim exactly between fork blades or between chain stays and seat stays.

6. Holding the wheel in place at the brake, first tighten the axle nuts one after the other by hand, then tighten them gradually with the wrench.

7. Verify you have installed the wheel in the right position and correct if necessary.

8. Tension the brake or reinstall the straddle cable's QR nipple, then readjust the brake to make sure the brake pads touch the sides of

Hold back the derailleur with the chain to remove and install the rear wheel.

the rim fully and equally when the brake lever is applied.

The Hub

Hubs should be checked occasionally to make sure they still turn freely and are not too loose. Maintenance will consist of adjustment, lubrication and overhauling when necessary. Cartridge hubs require specialized tools; some are adjustable.

You can maximize the life of a hub by means of regular checks, adjustment, lubrication and overhauling. To replace a hub, the entire wheel has to be rebuilt, which runs the bill up considerably. Besides, many models are only available as pairs, effectively doubling the cost.

Hub Bearing Check

This procedure applies to any kind of hub, whether it is the conventional adjustable bearing type or a cartridge bearing model.

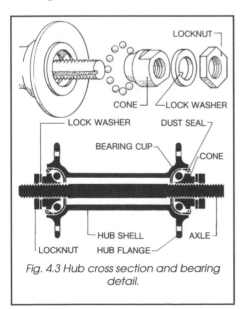

Fig. 4.3 Hub cross section and bearing detail.

Tools and equipment:
• Usually none required.

Procedure:

1. To check whether the hub runs freely, merely lift the wheel off the ground and let it spin slowly. It should rotate several times and then oscillate gradually into the motionless state with the (slightly heavier) valve at the bottom. If it does not turn freely, the bearings should be adjusted to loosen them (and probably they should be lubricated).

2. To check whether there is play in the bearings, grab the rim close to the brake with one hand, while holding at the fork or the stays with the other, and try to push it sideways in both directions. If it moves loosely, the bearing should be tightened somewhat.

Adjust Hub Bearings

Carry out this work when the preceding test indicates a need for readjustment. In the case of a rear hub, you may have to remove the freewheel block first to gain access to the RH bearing. Tighten the locknut on the drive side (RH side) firmly up against the underlying cone.

Tools and equipment:
• 13–16 mm cone wrenches
• 13–16 mm open ended wrenches

Procedure:

1. Remove the wheel or, if it has axle nuts, at least loosen the axle nut on one side if you want to leave the wheel installed on the bike.

2. Loosen the locknut on one side by one turn, countering by holding the cone on the same side of the wheel with the cone wrench.

3. Tighten or loosen the cone by about a quarter turn at a time until the bearing is just a little loose. To loosen, counter at the cone on the other side with an open-ended wrench. To tighten, counter at the *locknut* on the other side.

4. Hold the cone with the cone wrench and tighten the locknut hard up against it, which will slightly decrease the play.

5. Check and readjust if necessary.

6. Reinstall the wheel on the bike — or just tighten the axle nut if you loosened it on one side only.

Lubricate or Overhaul Hub

Once a season, or whenever adjusting will not solve the hub's problems, lubricate the hub in a big way as described here.

Tools and equipment:
- 13–16 mm cone wrenches
- 13–15 mm box or open-ended wrenches
- rags
- bearing grease

Dismantling procedure:

1. Remove the wheel from the bike.

2. Remove the quick-release or the axle nuts and washers.

3. Remove the locknut on one side, countering by holding the cone on the *same* side.

4. Lift off the lock washer.

5. Remove the cone, countering by holding the cone on the *other* side. Catch the bearing balls as you remove the cone.

6. Pull the axle (with the other cone, washer and locknut still installed at the other end) out of the hub

Hub bearing overhauling.
Left: holding back the cone while tightening or loosening the locknut.
right: removing the bearing cone.

shell, again catching the bearing balls and removing the plastic seal (if installed) from the hub shell.

Overhauling procedure:

1. Clean and inspect all bearing parts.

2. Replace the bearing balls with new ones of the same size, and replace any other parts that may be damaged. Damage is pitted, grooved or corroded surfaces.

Reassembly procedure:

1. First fill the clean bearing cups in the hub with bearing grease, then reinstall the dust seals.

2. Push the bearing balls into the grease, filling the circumference but leaving enough space to move freely. A rule of thumb is to use one ball less than might fill the cup.

3. Insert the axle with one cone, washer and locknut still installed. If you are working on a rear wheel, make sure it goes the same way round as it was originally.

4. Screw the other cone onto the free axle end, until the bearings seem just a little loose.

5. Install the lock washer with its key in the axle groove.

6. Screw the locknut on and tighten it against the cone.

7. Check and, if necessary, adjust the bearing as described above until it runs well.

8. Reinstall the wheel on the bike.

Notes:

1. If you replace the cones, make sure the axle protrudes equally far on both sides — reposition both cones and locknuts to achieve this if necessary.

2. Bearings that are packed with grease should not be lubricated with oil, because the oil would act more to flush out the grease than as a lubricant. However, some hub designs can be lubricated with a grease gun — this applies primarily to the Grease-Guard models made by SunTour for mountain bike use. Other hubs can be retrofitted with Grease-Guard fittings to achieve the same effect.

Rim and Spokes

These two parts have to be treated together, since the spoke tension

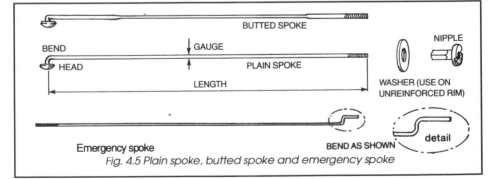

Fig. 4.5 Plain spoke, butted spoke and emergency spoke

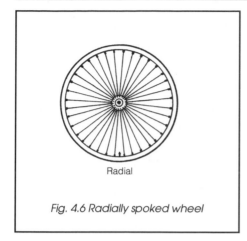

Radial

Fig. 4.6 Radially spoked wheel

determines largely whether the rim is straight and true or not. The spokes connect the rim to the hub in one of the patterns referred to as radial, 2-cross, 3-cross and 4-cross spoking, respectively. Almost any pattern is suitable for the front wheel, which does not transmit any torque; the rear wheel should have a 3- or 4-cross pattern, at least on the RH, or chain side. If you are a heavy rider or ride on rough roads, don't use wheels with fewer than 36 spokes — at least in the rear.

The way to minimize wheel problems, most typically broken spokes and bent rims, is to keep the spokes tensioned adequately. Check the feel and the sound of plucking a well-tensioned new wheel at a bike shop and compare yours. If necessary, increase the tension of all or some spokes, following the procedure outlined in the following section on wheel truing.

Wheel Truing Check

When a wheel is damaged, the rim is often permanently deformed sideways, resulting in wheel wobble.

This can be detected as lateral oscillations when riding. It may be verified by turning the wheel slowly while it is lifted off the ground, observing the distance between the rim and a fixed point on the frame's rear triangle or on the fork, for a rear wheel and a front wheel, respectively. On a properly trued wheel, this distance is the same on both sides of the wheel and does not vary as the wheel is turned.

Emergency Repair of Buckled Wheel

Sometimes the damage is so serious that you don't need to check: it will be obvious that the wheel is buckled — and there is little you can do to solve the problem permanently or even temporarily with adequate certainty to be safe. Just the same, such a seriously bent wheel can often be straightened enough to ride home — carefully.

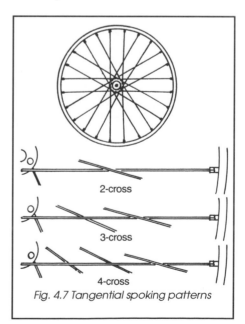

2-cross

3-cross

4-cross

Fig. 4.7 Tangential spoking patterns

Support the rim at the low point and push down forcefully on the high points. Check frequently and continue until the whole thing at least looks like a wheel. Then follow the procedure for *Wheel Trueing* to fine-tune the wheel far enough to be able to ride it home. Have it corrected or replaced as soon as possible.

Wheel Truing and Stress Relieving

This is the work done to get a bent wheel back into shape. It is most easily done at home, but can be carried out after a fashion by the roadside — at least well enough to get you home. In the home workshop, it is preferable to do this job using a truing stand, but it can be done with the wheel in the frame, preferably with the bike upside-down (but with the handlebars supported so nothing gets damaged). It will be best to remove the tire and the tube first, but this is not essential.

Tools and equipment:
• spoke wrench

Procedure:

1. Slowly spin the wheel while watching a fixed reference point on both sides, such as the gauge on the truing stand — or the bicycle's brake pads if you are working without a truing stand. Mark the locations that have to be moved further to the left and the right, respectively.

2. Using the nipple wrench, loosen the nipples of the spokes on the high side in the area of a high spot, and tighten those on the opposite side, in the same area. Turn the ones in the middle of the high spot ½ turn, and those further from the center only ¼ turn at a time (this is easy, since the nipples have a square flattened area for the tool).

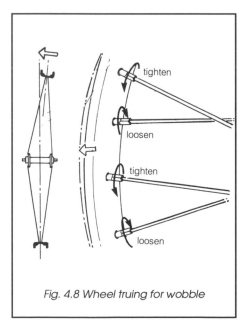

Fig. 4.8 Wheel truing for wobble

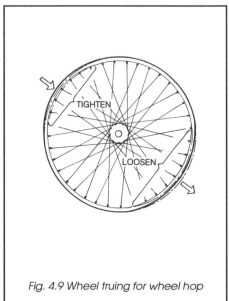

Fig. 4.9 Wheel truing for wheel hop

3. Your wheel must be properly centered once you have trued it. This is checked by using a special "dishing" tool or the brake pads for a reference point. If the wheel is off center, tighten all the spokes on one side in ¼-turn steps, and loosen the opposing spokes in ¼-turn steps to center the rim on the axle. Always begin and end at the valve hole so you don't miss any spokes.

4. Once you have achieved an improved spoke line, you must stress-relieve the spokes. This is done by grasping parallel spoke pairs on both sides of the wheel and squeezing them together working around the wheel, starting and finishing at the valve hole.

5. Continue this process for each off-set area, checking and correcting frequently, until the wheel is quite well trued.

6. On the rear wheel of a derailleur bike, the spokes on the RH side will be under a steeper angle, and consequently under a higher tension, than those on the LH side. This is on account of the asymmetry of the hub flanges owing to the freewheel block on the RH side.

Note:

The first time you true a wheel, it will take forever and a day and still may not lead to a really satisfactory result. Persist, and the next time will be easier. Just the same, the first few times you do this, have a bike mechanic check your work.

Replace Individual Spokes

Sometimes a spoke breaks — usually at the head, which is hooked in at the hub flange. Make sure you have re-

Using the spoke wrench

Replacing individual spokes

placement spokes of the same thickness and the same length.

Tools and equipment:
• nipple wrench
• tools to remove freewheel block or sprockets of cassette hub.

Procedure:

1. Remove freewheel block or freewheel cassette (refer to Chapter 6), tire, tube and rim tape. Unscrew nipple of broken spoke with nipple wrench.

2. Hook the spoke through the hole in the hub—with the head on the inside of the flange if this will be an outside spoke, on the outside if it will be an inside spoke.

3. Count four spokes along the circumference of the rim to find a spoke that is routed the same way as your spoke will have to be. Refer to this one to find out just how to run it and how it should cross which of the other spokes.

4. Route your spoke the same way as the example.

5. Screw the nipple onto the threaded end of the spoke, slowly increasing tension until it is about as tight as all other spokes on the same side of the same wheel.

6. Follow the procedure given under *Wheel Truing* until the wheel is perfectly true.

7. Replace tire, tube and rim tape. Inflate the tire.

Note:

If only one spoke is broken, and you don't have a spare spoke, true the wheel around the broken spoke by tightening and loosening the opposing sides. Stress-relieve the wheel, then true it again. If several spokes are broken, figure out which rim hole goes with which hub hole by observing that every fourth spoke along the rim (and every second one on the same hub flange, runs similarly.

Emergency Spoke Installation

Make your own emergency spoke by bending an oversized spoke from which you first remove the head to form a hook at one end (see Fig. 4.5). It is useful when a spoke on the RH side of the rear wheel breaks, since it can be hooked in without removing the freewheel.

Note:

When you get home, replace this temporary repair by a permanent spoke of the right length, a job you can either do yourself or leave to the bike shop. Warning: an improperly tensioned wheel can go out of true quickly or even collapse, especially if the spokes are too loose. Spokes tensioned too tightly will cause the rim to crack at the nipples.

Replace Rim

Here I will describe a simple method to replace a rim by a new one using the old hub and spokes. For a more thorough treatment, required when the spokes or the hub must also be replaced, see the following section *Wheel Building*.

Make sure the new rim is identical to the old one: Check the size and count the holes in the hub and the rim, and make sure the spoke holes are offset relative to the centerline of the rim in the same pattern (check on either side of the valve hole).

Tools and equipment:
- spoke wrench
- rag
- grease
- adhesive tape

Procedure:

1. Remove the tire, the tube and the rim tape from the old rim on the existing wheel.

2. Place the existing tape on the new rim, with the valve holes lined up.

3. Tape the two rims together between the spoke holes in at least three locations.

4. Starting at the first spoke to the right of the valve hole, remove each spoke from the old rim, and immediately install it in the new rim. Screw the nipple on until about 3 mm (⅛ in.) of the spoke screw thread is exposed.

5. After all the spokes have been replaced, work your way around the wheel, tightening all the spokes in steps of about one turn until they are equally tensioned.

6. Follow the description for wheel trueing to bring the wheel into lateral and radial true and to tension the spokes until they have about the same tension as those on a new wheel, paying attention to the need for higher tension on the freewheel side of a typical rear wheel.

7. Stress-relieve the spokes by grasping them in pairs of parallel spokes, working around the wheel. Center the wheel using a centering device if you have one, your brake pads if you do not. Ten-

Left: Push the spokes together to pull them in at the bend and relieve tensions at the nipple screw thread.

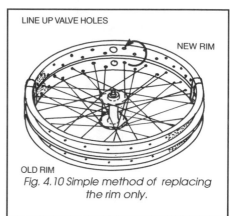

LINE UP VALVE HOLES

NEW RIM

OLD RIM

Fig. 4.10 Simple method of replacing the rim only.

sion and true the spokes again, if necessary.

8. Check inside the rim and file off any spoke ends that may project from the nipples.

9. Install the new rim tape, the tire and the tube. Inflate the tire and retrue the wheel, if necessary.

10. Check and retension the wheel every 50 km (30 miles) for the next 100 km (60 miles).

Wheel Building

This is the biggest wheel project, and it is one I only recommend you to do if you are really ambitious: a professional can do it so much faster that it is probably worth the money to have him do it. But it's wonderful therapy, and becomes easier as you do it more

A simple wheel truing stand for wheel building and truing.

often. Before you start, take a very close look at the old wheel (or another similar wheel) and the various descriptions and drawings in this chapter that show spoking details — try to understand what's going on before you start.

Spoke length determination:

Make sure you get the right spoke length — ask at the bike shop, telling them which hub and which rim you will be combining and which spoking pattern (radial, one-, two-, three-, or four-cross) you'll be using, and how many spokes will be used. Most wheels are built with 36 spokes, and for structural reasons I recommend using a four-cross pattern with low flange hubs (you'll be restricted to a maximum of three-cross when using high-flange hubs). On an off-set rear wheel (especially one used with a seven- or eight-speed freewheel block) the spokes on the RH side

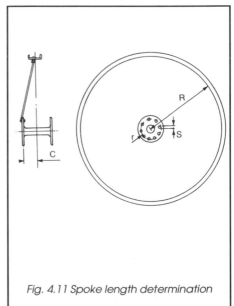

Fig. 4.11 Spoke length determination

should be about 3 mm (⅛ in.) shorter than those on the LH side; or, if you can't find the optimum spoke size, deviate a little on the low side for the spokes on the RH side, a little on the high side for the LH spokes.

If you are up to trigonometric calculations (or rather, if your hand-held calculator is), you may use the following formula to calculate the spoke length yourself (all dimensions in mm).

Spoke length = $\sqrt{(A^2 + B^2 + C^2)} - 0.5\,S$

where:

A = r sin (T)

B = R − r cos (T)

C = off-set from outside hub flange to center of wheel (measured as shown in Fig. 4.12, Detail A — on a front wheel, it is one half of thetotal hub width, on a rear   wheel it will be different on both sides)

r = ½ effective hub diameter (measured as shown in detail B)

R = ½ effective rim diameter (measured as shown in detail C)

T = 360 X/N

X = number of spoke crossings desired

N = number of spokes per hub flange (usually: one half total number of spokes)

S = spoke hole diameter in hub flange

If you have a programmable calculator (such as a Sharp Wizard), you can set up a little program to carry out the computation after entering the critical variables.

Spoke length check:

You will be excused if you're scared off by the formula in the preceding section. Alternatively, here's a method of determining relatively painlessly whether you are using the correct spoke length, based on the principle that any plane is determined by three points. Use this method whenever you are not absolutely sure whether you have the correct spoke length. You'll need only six spokes — check whether they are all equally long first: hold them upright on the table, screwed ends down, and compare the height of the heads. If the spoke length is found to be correct, you may continue spoking the entire wheel by the pattern thus established.

Tools and equipment:
• spoke wrench
• medium screwdriver
• lubricant (e.g. vaseline)
• rag

Procedure:

1. Take six spokes and nipples; lubricate the spoke ends and wipe off.

2. Hold the hub upright in front of you. On the upper hub flange, select three holes that are equally spaced (every sixth in the case of a 36-hole hub, which has 18 holes per flange; if the hub has more or less than 36 holes, you may not be able to space completely equally — just make sure the spokes are spaced as equally as possible, with

an odd number of empty spoke holes in the flange between the spokes). If the hub has holes that are alternately countersunk ('beveled'), select holes that are beveled on the inside. Put a spoke through each of these holes from the outside through to the inside.

3. Inspect the spoke holes in the rim: take the hole next to the valve hole that is off-set up (on most rims sold in the U.S. that is the first hole going counterclockwise, but it may also be the first one going clockwise, especially on Italian rims). Attach one of the three spokes with the nipple in this hole. Mark it with adhesive tape - we'll call it spoke 1 for later reference when completing the spoking pattern.

4. Count out the same number of holes that are off-set upward as there are vacant holes in the hub, going the same direction (clock-

wise or counterclockwise). Place the other two spokes in the corresponding holes determined this way. Now the spokes in the upper hub flange should be connected to similarly spaced holes that are off-set upward in the rim — correct if necessary.

5. Turn the wheel over, so that the hub flange without spokes faces up.

6. Visually line up the two hub flanges, noting how the holes in the near flange are positioned between the holes in the far flange. I'll call this offset from one hole in the one flange to the nearest hole in the other flange a "half space," while I'll call the space between consecutive holes in the same flange a "whole" space.

7. To find the location for the first spoke inserted on the flange that is on top now, read off the number of spaces from the table, as a func-

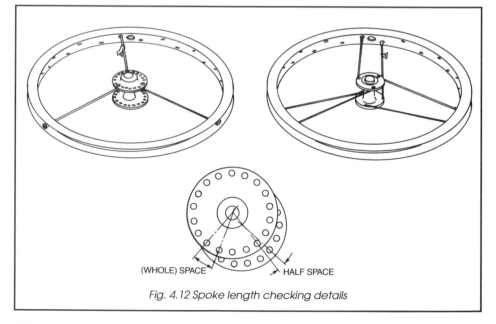

Fig. 4.12 Spoke length checking details

tion of the number of spokes and the number of spoke crossings required (e.g. 8 ½ for a four-cross pattern with 36 spokes). Count out the appropriate number of spaces from the hole where spoke 1 (marked with tape) is located in the direction of the valve hole (i.e. going counterclockwise if the valve hole is counterclockwise from the spoke). In the hub flange hole thus established, insert a spoke from the outside to the inside, and attach this spoke to the free spoke hole in the rim immediately adjacent to the valve hole.

8. Count out the same number of spoke holes in the hub on either side of this spoke as you count between corresponding spokes on the lower flange either side of spoke 1, inserting the two remaining spokes there, again from the outside to the inside.

9. Attach these spokes to the rim in the holes that are in the same relative position to each other as the two spokes on either side of the valve hole.

10. Stop to check whether you've got something that looks like the Fig. 4.13, and if not, where you went wrong. Correct anything that is amiss.

11. Tighten the six spokes gradually until the wheel is reasonably tight and centered (front wheel) or appropriately off-set ("dished" rear wheel) as required. If significant thread is exposed under the nipple (more than 1 thread), choose a **longer spoke**; if any part of the **spoke protrudes** beyond the nip-

ple inside the rim, choose a shorter spoke — and start all over again. If the spoke length is correct, continue building the wheel more or less as described in the following procedure *Spoking the Wheel*, starting at step 4.

Note:

If you are building a radially spoked (front) wheel, insert all spokes from the inside to the outside, so they all lie on the outside of the hub flanges.

Spoking the wheel:

This instruction is based on the assumption that you have determined the correct spoke length. If you're not sure, first carry out the check described above under *Spoke Length Check*, after which you'll be well on your way and can pick up the instructions starting at step 4. If you're rebuilding a wheel using an old hub or an old rim (or both), first cut away all the old spokes and remove them. If you're reusing the spokes and the hub, follow the earlier *Replace Rim*.

Tools and equipment:
• spoke wrench
• medium size screwdriver
• lubricant (e.g. vaseline)
• rag

Procedure:

1. Check whether all the spokes have the same length: take them all in your hand and push them ends-down on the table, and compare the heights of the heads. Lubricate the threaded ends and wipe of excess lubricant.

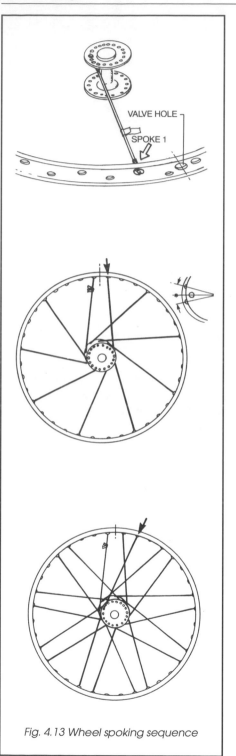

Fig. 4.13 Wheel spoking sequence

2. Take nine spokes (assuming a 36-spoke wheel — more or less for other wheels), and put one through every second hole in one of the hub flanges from the outside to the inside. If holes are alternately countersunk on the inside and the outside of the hub flange, select those holes that are countersunk on the inside.

3. Putting the hub in front of you, held vertically with the batch of spokes stuck through the upper flange, find the spoke hole in the hub that's immediately next to the valve hole and is off-set upward. Take one spoke and attach it with the nipple to that hole; mark this spoke (e.g. with tape). I'll refer to it as *spoke 1*. Screw on the nipple about five turns.

4. Similarly attach the other spokes so far installed in the hub into every fourth hole in the rim. If you followed the instruction *Spoke Length Check* above, just put in the remaining spokes — you already have three of them.

5. Check to make sure all these spokes are attached to spoke holes that are off-set upward in the rim, and that three free spoke holes remain between each pair of consecutive spokes in the rim, one free hole in the hub.

6. Turn the wheel over and establish whether the remaining free hole immediately next to the valve hole is oriented clockwise or counterclockwise. Select the spoke holes in the flange now nearest to you that are each off-set half a space from the spokes already installed

on the far flange in that same direction. Insert the next set of nine (or whatever is the appropriate number) spokes in these holes, leaving a free hole between each set of consecutive spokes.

7. Locate spoke 1 (the one on the far flange next to the valve hole) and count out the appropriate number of spaces to determine where the next spoke is, which you'll attach in the free spoke hole on the other side of the valve hole, counting clockwise if the free spoke hole is also clockwise from the valve hole, counterclockwise if the free hole is counterclockwise from the valve hole. If you followed the instruction *Spoke Length Check* this has already been determined — just install the missing spokes.

8. Attach the remaining spokes so far inserted in the hub into every fourth spoke hole in the rim.

9. You should now have sets of two spokes, each set separated by two free holes in the rim and by one free hole in the hub flanges. Make

any corrections that may be required.

10. Insert the next batch of spokes from the inside to the outside in one of the hub flanges.

11. Take any one of these spokes and 'lace' it to cross the chosen number of spokes on the same hub flange for the crossing pattern selected, always crossing under the last one. If you're building a four-cross wheel, that will be over the first, over the second, over the third and then forced under the fourth. Attach this spoke in the next free hole in the rim that's offset in the corresponding direction. If it doesn't fit, you either have the wrong spoke length for the pattern selected, have tightened the other spokes too much (rarely the case), or you made a mistake somewhere along the line — check and restart if necessary.

12. Do the same with the last batch of spokes, inserting them in the free holes in the other hub flange from the inside to the outside, making

No. of spokes in wheel	1-cross angle	spaces	2-cross angle	spaces	3-cross angle	spaces	4-cross angle	spaces	5-cross angle	spaces
24	75°	2½	135°	4½	–	–	–	–	–	–
28	64.3°	2½	115.7°	4½	167.1°	6½	–	–	–	–
32	56.3°	2½	101.3°	4½	146.3°	6½	–	–	–	–
36	50°	2½	90°	4½	130°	6½	170°	8½	–	–
40	45°	2½	81°	4½	117°	6½	153°	8½	–	–
44	40.9°	2½	73.6°	4½	106.4°	6½	139.1°	8½	171.8°	10½
48	37.5°	2½	67.5°	4½	97.5°	6½	127.5°	8½	157.5°	10½

Table 4-I. Spoke hole spacing in hub for neighboring spokes in rim

the right crossings; then install them in the remaining spoke holes in the rim.

13. You now have a complete, but loosely spoked, wheel. Once more check to make sure the pattern is correct as you intended, then start tightening the spoke nipples progressively, working around several times, first using the screwdriver, then — when the nipples begin to get tighter — with the spoke wrench. Don't tighten too much though: it should remain easy to turn the nipples with the spoke wrench.

14. Check whether the wheel is correctly centered between the locknuts at the wheel axle, as outlined in step 3 of the description *Wheel Truing* above and the subsequent note.

15. Install the wheel in the bike, which should be hung up off the ground by saddle and handlebars or placed upside-down (taking care to support it at the handlebars so nothing gets damaged), and make the same kind of corrections as outlined under *Wheel Truing* above, until the wheel is perfectly round and has no lateral deflection.

16. Proceed to tighten the spokes all around equally. Unless you're an experienced piano-tuner, it's hard to explain in writing how tight is right. Just compare with another good wheel (ask in the bike shop) to develop a feel for the right tension. Tension is checked by pushing spokes together in crossed

pairs at a point between the rim and the last cross. On an offset rear wheel, the RH spokes (chain side) should be considerably tighter than those on the other side. All the spokes on the same side of a wheel must be equally tight.

17. Now take spokes together in sets of four — two nearby sets of crossed spokes on each side of the wheel — at the point of their last crossing and squeeze them together quite forcefully. This will bend the spokes into their final shape and release all sorts of built-up stresses, resulting in some disturbing sounds. Don't be perturbed — if you don't do this now it will happen while you're riding the bike, when it's too late to make the required corrections.

18. After this stress-relieving operation, check the wheel for roundness and tightness once more — you will probably have to tighten several spokes a little more, since they have staightened and some will have partly 'unwound' from their nipples.

19. After perhaps 40 km (25 miles) of cycling, check and true the wheel once more. It's a lot of work, but think of the satisfaction.

Note:

A radially spoked wheel (sometimes used for a front wheel) is simpler, since all spokes can be inserted from the inside to the outside, finishing up on the outside of the hub flanges of the finished wheel.

CHAPTER 5

Tires and Tubes

The tires remain the bicycle's weak spot. I advise carrying a spare tube, a pump and a repair kit at all times. Two different categories of tires are in use for bicycles: the wired-on tire, consisting of separate cover and inner tube, and the tubular tire (referred to as tub in Britain, sew-up in the U.S.). The latter type is primarily used in bicycle racing; the former is the more universally used.

Tire Size

Tire and rim must be matched: narrow sprint rims are used to mount tubular tires. Many different diameters and widths of Endrick rims are available — as well as matching tires.

In general, wider and heavier tires are used for poorer road surfaces. Until the early 80s, the most common size was 27 × 1¼ in. (nominally — in reality most models so designated are actually considerably narrower).

Nowadays the French 700 C size is used pretty universally for drop-handlebar bicycles. Whereas the 27-in. tire is mounted on rims of 630 mm tire seat (or rim shoulder) diameter, the 700 C tire fits on a 622 mm tire seat diameter. For mountain bikes, the most popular sizes are 26 × 2.125 and 26 × 1.75 in., both mounted on 559 mm tire seat diameter rims. British 26-in. tires are much narrower and are not interchangeable with the American size; they are mounted on rims with a tire seat diameter of 584 mm. French 650 B tires are also somewhat similar in size to 26-in. tires, but again narrower (though still thicker than the British 26-in. models) and are mounted on rims with a tire seat diameter of 671 mm. Hybrids, finally usually come equipped with 700 B tires, which fit on a wider version of the 622 mm rim.

This is about as far as I can go on the subject of tire sizing in what must primarily remain a repair manual. In the remaining sections of this chapter I shall cover the various repair and replacement jobs associated with tires, tubes and tubular tires.

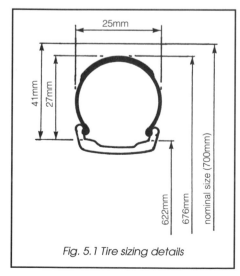

Fig. 5.1 Tire sizing details

Puncture Repair

More commonly referred to as "fixing a flat" in the U.S., this work is required more frequently than any

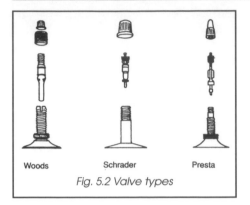

Woods   Schrader   Presta

Fig. 5.2 Valve types

other repair, and every cyclist should
be able to handle this simple job.
Whether you actually repair the old
tube or install a new one is up to you,
but you can't carry unlimited spares,
so you will be confronted with the
need to repair the leak yourself
sooner or later. Though the description involves many steps, the work is
not difficult and can, with some practice, be handled in about ten minutes,
even out on the trail.

The whole thing is expedited considerably if the tire and rim match
rather generously. That is typically
taken care of by selecting rims with a
deep bed and trying out the tire for
fit. In fact, on mountain bikes, it is
often possible to remove the tire by
hand without the need for tire levers.

Tools and equipment:
- tire repair kit
- tire levers
- spare tube
- 13–15 mm wrench
- small screwdriver

Procedure:

1. Check the valve. Try to inflate and
    check whether air is escaping
    there. Sometimes a Schrader valve
    will leak and can be fixed by

screwing in the interior, using a
narrow object, like a small
screwdriver. Presta valves will
leak if the top nut isn't screwed on.

2. Remove the wheel from the bike,
    holding back chain and rear derail-
    leur, after having selected a gear
    that combines a small cog with a
    small chainring if you're dealing
    with a rear wheel. If necessary to
    clear the brakes, either push the
    (limp) tire together locally, or
    release the brake cable.

3. Check the circumference of the tire
    for visible signs of damage, and
    mark their location with a
    ballpoint pen or by tying some-
    thing around the nearest spoke.

4. If the tire still contains air, push
    the valve pin in (Schrader), or first
    unscrew the nut, then push the
    valve pin in (Presta). This will
    allow all trapped air to escape.

5. To loosen the tire, push one side of
    the tire towards the (deeper) cen-

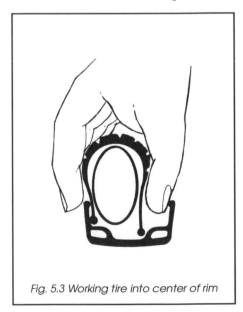

Fig. 5.3 Working tire into center of rim

ter of the rim around the entire circumference of the wheel to loosen
that side enough to ease removal.

6. If it does not come off by hand,
    place the longer end of a tire lever
    under the side of the tire and hook
    the short end under a spoke.

7. Two or three spokes further round
    the rim, insert the second tire lever.

8. If necessary, insert the third tire
    lever two or three spokes in the
    opposite direction (if it is neces-
    sary and you have only two
    levers, remove one of the two and
    use it in the new location).

9. Remove the tire levers and pull
    the rest of that side of the tire off
    by hand, working around, starting
    at the location of the tire levers.

10. Remove the tube from under the
    tire, pushing the valve out of the
    valve hole.

*Insert the tire levers carefully to avoid
pinching the inner tube as you do so.*

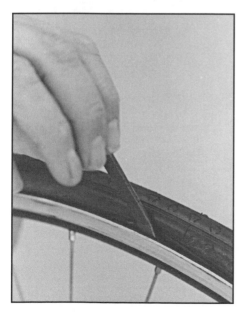

11. Check the tube, starting at any
    location you may have marked as
    an obvious or probable cause of
    the puncture.

12. If the leak is not easily detected, in-
    flate the tire and check carefully
    for escaping air, passing the tube
    by your eye, which is your most
    sensitive detection device. To date,
    I have not encountered a leak that
    could not be found this way, but it
    takes some practice.

13. If you are not able to detect escap-
    ing air, submerge the inflated tire
    in water or, if not enough of that is
    available, rub a little water from
    your water bottle over the inflated
    tire, systematically working
    around and reinflating the tire as
    required to maintain adequate
    pressure.

14. Mark the location of the leak.

15. Take an appropriate patch from
    the patch kit. Generally, the smal-
    lest size will do, except if you are
    dealing with several holes close
    together or with a long tear.

16. If necessary, dry the tube around
    the leak. Roughen the area around
    the leak with sandpaper from the
    patch kit and wipe clean.

17. Take a sizeable drop of rubber
    solution from the tube in the patch
    kit and quickly spread it smoothly
    and evenly over an area around
    the leak that is a little larger than
    the patch.

18. Allow the rubber solution to dry
    one minute for a normal butyl
    tube, twice that long if you have a
    latex tube.

19. Remove the plastic or aluminum foil from the adhesive side of the patch without touching the adhesive, and quickly yet accurately place the patch on the area prepared, centered at the leak.

20. Push the patch down, then knead and flex patch and tube together to make sure the patch adheres fully. If not, remove it and restart at step 15.

21. Inflate the tube partway to establish whether air escapes. If it does, there may be another hole or the first one was not patched properly. Repeat the repair if necessary.

22. After you have inflated the tube, while waiting to verify whether it holds air, check the inside of the tire to find and remove any embedded objects that may have caused the puncture — or may cause subsequent ones. Particularly tricky in off-road cycling are thorns, which wear off to be invisible on the outside, yet protrude far enough inside to pierce the tube when the tire is compressed.

23. Also check inside the rim well to make sure none of the spokes protrude and that they are covered by rim tape. Once at home, file off any spokes that do protrude, and replace or patch defective rim tape. Duct tape works nicely.

24. When you are sure the problem is solved, let most of the air escape from the tube until it is limp.

25. Starting at the valve, put the tube back under the tire, over the rim.

26. Starting opposite the valve and working in both directions towards it, carefully pull the side of the tire back over the rim.

27. If the tube has a Presta valve, reinstall the knurled locknut. Whatever the valve, make sure it is straight.

28. Inflate the tire partway and check once more to make sure the tube is not pinched, kneading the tire sidewalls from both sides, and making sure it is centered. The ridge on the side should be equally far from the rim around the circumference on both sides.

29. Inflate the tire to the desired pressure — the narrower the tire, the higher the pressure should be.

Lift the tire casing off the rim towards the other side, and push the valve up through the valve hole in the rim.

Note:

Even if you choose not to patch a tube while you are out on the road, replacing it with your spare tube instead, you should repair the puncture once you get home, so you can use that tube as a spare.

Replace Inner Tube or Tire Casing

If the inner tube cannot be repaired, because the hole is on a seam or too large, or if you want to install another tube for any other reason, proceed as described above for repairing a puncture under steps 2–10, then install the new tube and continue as described under steps 25–29.

To replace the tire casing itself, initially also proceed as described above in steps 2–10 for repairing a puncture. Then remove the other side of the tire in the same direction as the first side. Put one side of the new tire in place and continue as before.

Patching Tire Casing

Sometimes a tire casing that is damaged can be repaired at least temporarily. To do so, proceed just as you did for the puncture repair. Repair the inside of the tire, using a 2.5 x 5 cm (1 × 2 in.) "boot." This can be a piece of duct tape, a piece cut from the side of a discarded lightweight tire, or even a piece of plastic sheet if you're desperate. First put rubber solution on one side of the patch, allowing it to dry, and then reapply rubber solution there and in the area of the tire where it has to be repaired. Once it has adhered, generously sprinkle talcum powder

over the area of the boot and around it to prevent the tire from sticking to the tube.

Tire Sealants and Other Tricks

Every few years some manufacturer claims to have solved the problem of the flat tire forever. The proposed solutions fall into three different categories: more or less solid tubes, tube sealants, and reinforced tire casings. All of them have some effect, but to date the perfect solution has not been offered.

The use of a sticky sealant, advertised under the name Green Slime in the U.S., has proven very effective against the problems associated with a straightforward puncture caused by glass or other sharp objects. Similar to the compound used to seal tubeless car tires, it builds up a sealing layer around and over the point where a leak starts to develop. I have never had a need for it (I get very few punctures because I ride carefully, and avoid bad roads), but if you tend to get many punctures, you should probably invest in a bottle and squirt it into the tire while inflating it.

Solid inner tubes have been offered before, but the current crop is more interesting. Consisting of a plastic closed-cell foam material, it is relatively light and flexible. Even the best of these things feel more dead than conventional pneumatic tires, and they are comfortable mainly where they are least needed — namely on perfectly smooth roads. On rough roads their harshness soon becomes very uncomfortable.

Finally there are reinforced, or belted, tire casings. Typically these include a strip of very strong but reasonably flexible woven material between the regular casing fabric and the rubber tread. Even these only prevent straight punctures, while they are of little or no help against the pervasive snakebite punctures, which are attributable to pinching the tube between the rim and the tire casing when riding over an obstacle. By and large, the most effective preventive measures remain careful riding and adequate inflation pressure.

Replace Valve

Although most people will replace a tube if it is damaged near the valve or if the valve itself is leaking, it is possible to make a repair at this point, provided the valve is not vulcanized or moulded together with the tube, but screwed on. Nowadays all regular tubes have vulcanized valves, but you can still do this work as long as you have an old valve to use. Sew-ups (tubular tires) still come with screwed-on valves, so a good source is any discarded sew-up from any bike shop's garbage can. Remove the defective valve, then mend the hole with a big patch as though it

were a regular puncture. Put a big patch on the tube in some other suitable location for the valve; carefully cut a small hole in the middle, going through the patch and the tube. Work the base of the valve through this hole, and clamp down the valve with the washer and the small hexagonal locknut that held the valve in place on the original tube. Inflate and check — correct if necessary.

Tubular Tires (Sew-Ups)

These special racing tires are used less today than they once were, mainly due to the inconvenience of repairing them. They are sewn around their tube and literally glued to a special rim. Although modern high-pressure wired-on tires are almost as light and the rolling resistance on most surfaces can be equally low, some riders still prefer tubular tires. Because they don't sit in a deep-bedded rim with sharp edges, they are actually less sensitive to so-called snakebite punctures so common amongst inexperienced riders with wired-on tires.

Patching a tubular tire, or sew-up, is a work of love — if you have

Once you have made sure the inner tube is not trapped, pull the tire casing back over the rim.

neither the patience to do it, nor the money to have someone else do it for you or to buy a new one each time you have a puncture, you'd be better off installing wired-on tires and the matching rims.

Remove Tubular Tire

To remove the tire when you have a puncture, first remove the wheel from the bike. Starting opposite the valve, roll off the tire with the palms of both hand, working around the tire in both directions; finally, remove the valve from the rim. When folding up the tire, take care to do it in such a way that the adhesive backing does not stick together.

Install Tubular Tire

When you have a puncture on the way, it is perfectly satisfactory to simply install the spare on the still tacky rim, merely taking care not to corner so wildly that the thing might come off. For a permanent installation, proceed as follows:

Tools and equipment:
• either: tube of tire adhesive, or: double-sided adhesive tire-mounting tape (the latter is easier to use; it is, however, hard to get in parts of the U.S., though readily available elsewhere)
• acetone or other solvent
• pump

Procedure:
1. Clean off the old adhesive with acetone or remove the old adhesive tape.

2. When using adhesive compound: spread an even layer on the entire rim bed, subsequently cleaning your hands either with acetone or (preferably) with waterless hand cleaner.

3. When using adhesive tape: wrap the tape around the rim tightly, starting just before the valve hole and ending just after (i.e. overlapping at the valve hole), centering the tape carefully. Push it down with a firm rounded object like the handle of a screwdriver. Cut a hole for the valve, then remove the paper backing strip, also from the overlapped part.

4. Slightly moisten the adhesive rim bed, so the tire does not adhere, fully before it is properly positioned. Place a strip of paper, about two inches wide, opposite the valve hole; this will give you a good place to start removal of the tire when it has to be replaced later.

5. Inflate the tire somewhat. If you're installing a brand new tire, first stretch it, holding it down with

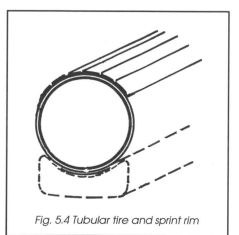

Fig. 5.4 Tubular tire and sprint rim

your feet, as you pull the opposite end up forcefully with your hands.

6. Insert the valve, then place the tire on the rim, centering it properly as you work all around the rim (compare the concentricity of the sidewall).

7. Inflate to the final pressure, then check and correct concentricity once more. Remove any spilled adhesive and tear off the ends of the paper strip opposite the valve. Wait at least overnight before using the wheel, so the adhesive will be cured.

Repair Tubular Tire

The instructions that follow are based on the assumption that the tire has been removed from the wheel — it's not a roadside repair but one to do at home.

Tools and equipment:
• tubular tire patch kit (comprising patches, rubber solution, sandpaper, twine, needle, thimble, and talcum powder (often in the form of a stick which you scrape to obtain powder)
• sharp knife
• pump

Procedure:

1. Inflate the tire to find out where the hole is. Listen or, if you don't hear escaping air, pass the entire tire surface closely past your eyes, which are very sensitive; if this doesn't work either, submerge the tire in water, a section at a time, watching for escaping air bubbles. Mark the location of the leak.

2. Over an area about 4–5 inches either side of the leak, remove the backing tape, using a thin object.

3. Draw a ball-point line every half inch across the seam in the tire, then cut away the stitching over a length of about 6 inches, centered about the leak. Remove the loose remains of the stitching.

4. Dig the tube out from under the backing strip; repair the puncture as described for a regular puncture in *Puncture Repair*, steps 10–24 above.

5. Put the tube back in the cover, and pull the backing tape and the cover itself together, lining up the lines you had drawn before.

6. Holding back the tube so it will not get damaged, carefully sew together the seam, not pulling it so tight that it will not lie flat. Work the ends of the twine back under the stitching to prevent it from unraveling.

7. Using the regular rubber solution on the tire cover and the cover tape, glue the tape back into place.

Note:

Keep spare tubular tires in a cool dry place, preferably inflated somewhat, and best of all installed around a spare rim. Don't forget to pack a spare when riding; release it from its tightly folded position for proper storage when you get home.

CHAPTER 6

The Drivetrain

The bicycle's drivetrain comprises the parts that transmit the rider's legwork to the rear wheel. They are the bottom bracket with cranks and chainrings, the pedals, the chain, and the freewheel block with cogs. The derailleurs, which are sometimes considered part of the drive-train, are covered separately in Chapter 7, which is devoted to the derailleur gearing system.

The Cranks

Virtually all modern bicycles are equipped with aluminum cotterless cranks, while cottered and one-piece models have become quite rare. Cotterless cranks are held onto square tapered ends of the spindle by a matching square tapered hole and a bolt or nut, depending on the design of the spindle. Since those held with bolts are usually better than those held with nuts, choose the former when replacing a bottom bracket.

The bolt or nut is covered by a dustcap, which protects the screw thread in the recess. This screw thread is used to pull the crank off the spindle for maintenance or re-

placement by means of a crank extractor tool. The RH crank has an attachment spider or ring, to which the chainrings are bolted.

The crank extractor consists of two parts, which may be permanently combined: a wrench for the crank bolt and the actual extractor. Crank bolts come in sizes 14–16 mm; most quality bikes use 15 mm crank bolts, cheaper models use 14 mm, while TA and Stronglight use 16 mm. The crank extractor fits into the threaded hole surrounding the crank bolt, and pulls the crank off its spindle when it is tightened. For the 22 mm threaded holes found on most bikes, I recommend the Campagnolo tool, which has a separate long-handled wrench.

The parts of the drivetrain on a mountain bike. Also shown here are the major components of a derailleur gearing system, which will be covered in Chapter 7.

TA and Stronglight cranks have 23 mm threaded holes and require a specific tool.

Some Campagnolo and older Shimano chain-sets do not use conventional crank bolts, but a one-key release system. These require only one Allen key (6 mm for Shimano and 7 mm for Campagnolo) to both loosen the crank and pull it off the spindle. Whatever you do, don't attempt to remove the insert from the crank. If it becomes loose, you must take it out, clean the screw thread, and cement it in place with an anaerobic locking adhesive, such as Loctite blue.

A new bike's cranks should be tightened every 40 km (25 miles) for the first 200 km (125 miles), since initially the soft aluminum of the cranks deforms so much that the connection between the spindle and the crank tends to come loose. This is the reason you should carry the crank bolt wrench tool in your repair kit. Beyond that, the crank is merely removed when it is damaged or when you have to adjust or overhaul the bottom bracket.

It is not uncommon in off-road cycling to bend a crank during a fall. Before you replace the entire crank, let a bike mechanic try to straighten it out. This requires a special tool that is not worth buying for the average home mechanic.

Replace Cotterless Crank

This job is necessary when a crank or an entire chain-set has to be replaced. It also has to be done for many maintenance jobs on the bottom bracket.

Tools and equipment:
• 4–7 mm Allen key
• adjustable pin wrench
• crank extractor
• crank bolt wrench
• rag
• grease

Removal procedure:

1. Remove the dustcap, which can generally be done with a coin, though some models require the use of an Allen key or adjustable pin wrench. (Some recent Shimano versions have Allen crank bolts with a flexible grommet, eliminating the need for a separate dustcap.

2. Unscrew the bolt or the nut with the wrench part of the crank tool, while holding the crank firmly.

3. Remove the washer that lies under the bolt or nut. This is an important step; if you forget to do this, you will not be able to remove the crank, but will damage it.

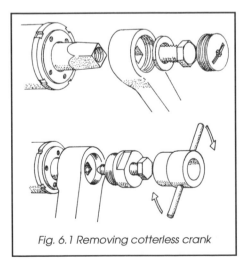

Fig. 6.1 Removing cotterless crank

4. Make sure the internal part of the crank extractor is retracted as far as it will go.

5. Dab a little grease on the crank extractor tool's threads, then screw it into the threaded recess in the crank by at least three full turns, preferably more.

6. Holding the crank with one hand to counter, turn the handle of the crank extractor (or the wrench that fits on it instead of a handle on some models) in. This will eventually pull the crank off the spindle.

7. Remove the tool from the crank.

Installation procedure:

1. Clean the matching surfaces of the spindle and the crank hole, then

Hold the crank back and screw in the center of the crank puller.

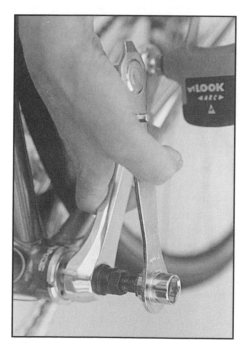

apply a thin layer of grease to these surfaces.

2. Push the crank onto the spindle, making sure the two cranks are 180 degrees off-set and that the crank with the attachment for the chainrings goes on the RH side.

3. Install the washer.

4. Install the bolt or the nut and tighten it fully, then install the dust cap.

5. Firmly retighten the connection after about 40 km (25 miles).

One-key release models

Some cotterless crank-sets are equipped with a one-key release system, which can be operated with a single Allen key without the need for a special extractor. Here the crank attachment bolt is in the form of an Allen bolt; the place of the dustcap is taken by a stronger screwed insert with LH thread, installed with a special pin wrench and held in place with locking adhesive. When the bolt, which is accessible through a

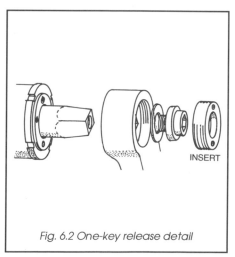

Fig. 6.2 One-key release detail

hole in this insert, is unscrewed, its head soon hits the inside of the insert and forces the crank off the spindle as it is unscrewed further.

Installation is just as simple: place the crank on the axle, making sure to line up the screwed end of the bolt with the screwed hole in the axle; then tighten the bolt. If the insert gives the slightest hint of coming loose, take it out, clean the screw thread, and cement it in with anaerobic locking adhesive. If the insert were lost, you would find it impossible to remove the crank.

Cottered Cranks

See Fig. 6.3 for this type of attachment, which is still used on low-end bikes (and on some perfectly good older machines). If the crank comes loose, tighten the nut. If the problem persists (or to replace the crank), remove the nut and hammer out the cotter pin, while supporting the crank on something solid. When replacing the cotter pin, take the old one to the shop to make sure you get the right size.

Tools and equipment:
• wrench to fit nut on cotter pin
• hammer
• something solid to support crank

Removal procedure:

1. Unscrew nut on cotter pin until the end of the cotter pin is about 1.5 mm (¹⁄₁₆ in.) below the top of the nut, or by at least two full turns, whichever is more.

2. Supporting the crank with something solid, hammer down the nut until it touches the crank.

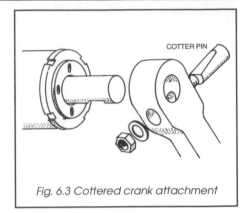

Fig. 6.3 Cottered crank attachment

3. Unscrew the nut completely and push or hammer the cotter pin out; remove the crank.

Installation procedure:

1. Place the crank on the spindle. Note that the hole in the crank must be lined up with the groove in the spindle, and that the crank with the chainwheel or the attachment for the chainwheel is on the RH side (chain side) of the bike.

2. Place the cotter pin through the crank from the bigger hole (assuming one of the holes is bigger, which can easily be verified by trying to put the cotter pin in from both sides). The flat side of the cotter pin must be aligned with the groove in the spindle.

3. Supporting the crank with something solid, hammer the cotton pin in until enough screw thread protrudes to install the washer and the nut, then tighten the nut fully; hammer down and tighten again.

Note:

If the cotter pin is damaged or if the thread is worn so much that the nut feels loose, it should be replaced by one of the same diameter (several different diameters are in use) although, by way of temporary repair, installing a second nut (locknut) may do the trick. Filing the flat face down until it is smooth will be sufficient if the cotter pin is not too seriously deformed. Tighten again after about 40 km (25 miles) of use. If for some reason the crank must be replaced, make sure to get one for the same spindle diameter and the same pedal thread size (see instructions for pedal replacement elsewhere in this chapter).

The Bottom Bracket

This is the heart of the drivetrain, installed in the frame's bottom bracket shell. It is made up of the spindle, or axle, to which the cranks are attached, and the ball bearings that allow it to turn smoothly. The conventional, or BSA, type has adjustable bearings, whereas the bearings of the cartridge (or sealed) unit are not adjustable, although some models can be adjusted laterally to improve the chain line.

If a cartridge bottom bracket develops play or tightness, the bearing cartridges have to be replaced. Except for special models that are easily removable, you may have to take the bike to a shop to have it overhauled or replaced.

Adjust Bottom Bracket

Carry out this work on a conventional bottom bracket when the bearings have developed play or when they are too tight.

Tools and equipment:
• bottom bracket tools (special wrenches for the lockring and the bearing cups)

Procedure:

1. Unless it is a model with an adjustable cup with flats for use of a wrench, remove the LH crank.

2. Loosen the lockring on the LH side by about one half turn.

3. Loosen the adjustable bearing cup by turning it a quarter turn counterclockwise if the bearing is too tight, clockwise if it is too loose.

4. Restraining the bearing cup, tighten the lockring, then repeat

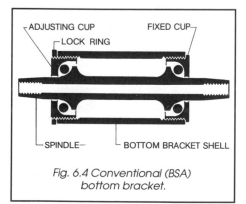

Fig. 6.4 Conventional (BSA) bottom bracket.

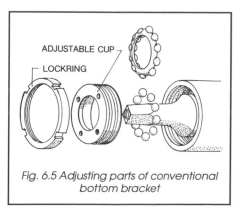

Fig. 6.5 Adjusting parts of conventional bottom bracket

to fine-tune the adjustment if necessary.

Notes:

☐ Bottom bracket looseness is best detected with the cranks installed, using them for leverage while twisting sideways.

☐ Tightness is best established when the cranks are removed.

☐ If you can get the pin wrench for the adjustable cup ground down so it fits between the crank and the cup, it will be possible to carry out this adjustment without removing the LH crank.

Overhaul Bottom Bracket

This description applies to conventional bottom brackets. Cartridge-bearing bottom brackets vary from

Overhauling the bottom bracket. After the cranks have been removed, remove first the lockring and then the bearing cup on the LH side, giving access to the bearings and the spindle.

one model to the next and usually require special tools — refer any problems to the bike shop. Other models will be treated separately.

Tools and equipment:
• crank bolt wrench
• crank extractor
• bottom bracket tools
• rags
• solvent
• bearing grease

Dismantling procedure:

1. Remove the LH and RH cranks.

2. Loosen and remove the lockring on the LH side.

3. Loosen and remove the adjustable bearing cup with the pin wrench (or, on older models, with a matching thin open-ended wrench), catching the bearing balls which are usually held in a retainer.

4. Pull the spindle out, also catching the bearing balls on the other side.

Overhauling procedure:

1. Clean and inspect all parts, watching for corrosion, wear and damage — grooved or pitted bearing surfaces.

2. If there is serious damage or wear, also check the condition of the fixed (RH) bearing cup, which otherwise remains on the bike. Except on some imported French and Italian bikes (which have RH thread), the fixed cup invariably has LH threading.

3. Replace any parts that are visibly corroded, damaged or worn, taking the old parts to the shop

with you to make sure you get matching replacements.

Installation procedure:

1. Pack both cleaned bearing cups with bearing grease.

2. If the fixed bearing cup has been removed, reinstall it, turning it counterclockwise.

3. Push the bearing ball retainers into the grease-filled bearing cups, making sure they are such a way round that only the balls — not the metal of the retainer — contact the cup.

4. Put the spindle in from the LH side — with the longer end (for the chainring side) first, if it is not symmetrical.

5. Install the adjustable cup with its bearing ball retainer in place.

6. Install the lockring.

7. Adjust the bearing as described in the preceding description until it runs smoothly and without play.

Lateral Adjustment of Cartridge Bottom Bracket

Although the bearings of these units usually cannot be adjusted to compensate for play or wear, at least the screw threaded versions allow something that cannot easily be done with other bottom brackets: their lateral position relative to the centerline of the bike can be adjusted. This makes it relatively easy to correct the chain line (the alignment of chainring and cog, which will be covered below). You will need the special lockring wrenches for the unit in question. Just loosen the one lockring and tighten the other one until the bearing unit is moved over sideways into the desired position.

Bottom Bracket with One-Piece Crank

One-piece cranks are traditionally popular on cheaper American bicycles. Fig. 6.7 shows how this type of bottom bracket is installed. Here

Left: Lateral adjustment of cartridge bottom bracket.

OUTER RACE
INNER RACE

Fig. 6.6 Cartridge bottom bracket

the bearing cups are pushed into the ends of the bottom bracket shell, and adjustable cones are screwed on the spindle, which forms one integral part with the two cranks. To adjust, proceed as follows:

Tools and equipment:
• medium size screwdriver
• wrench to fit locknut on LH side

Adjusting procedure:

1. Loosen the locknut on the LH side by turning it to the right (it has LH thread) while holding the crank.

2. Lift the lock washer and turn the underlying cone with the screwdriver to the right to loosen, or to the left to tighten, the bearing.

3. Hold the cone in place while tightening the locknut to the left.

Overhaul Bottom Bracket with One-Piece Crank

Tools and equipment:
• medium size screwdriver
• wrench to fit locknut

• wrench to fit cone on chainwheel side
• large screwdriver (if cups must be replaced)
• hammer (if cups must be replaced)
• block of wood (if cups must be replaced)
• bearing grease
• rag

Disassembly procedure:

1. Remove the LH pedal (see elsewhere in this chapter)

2. Unscrew the LH locknut to the right (LH screw thread) and remove locknut and lock washer.

3. Unscrew the adjustable (LH) cone, and remove the cone and the bearing retainer.

4. Wriggle the chainring out free from the chain and pull the entire Z-shaped crank unit out towards the RH (chain) side of the bike.

5. Remove the bearing retainer of the RH side bearing.

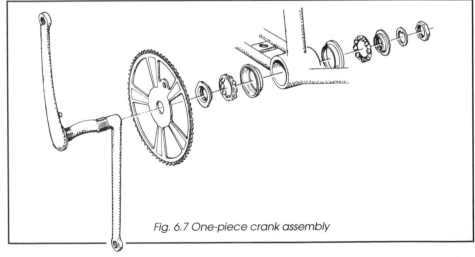

Fig. 6.7 One-piece crank assembly

6. Inspect all parts; replace the bearing ball retainers and any parts that are grooved, pitted or corroded.

Note:

The RH cone can be removed by simply unscrewing it, which will also loosen the chainring. The bearing cups can be removed by hammering them out, using the large screwdriver. Follow the illustration for reinstallation; the cups must be driven home until they are firmly seated.

Assembly procedure

1. Start reassembling after cleaning and lubricating all parts; put bearing grease in both cups, then screw the fixed cone back up over the chain-wheel on the RH crank.

2. Install the bearing ball retainer in the RH cup, then insert the crank unit from the RH side.

3. Install the LH bearing retainer in the grease-packed LH cup: screw the adjustable cone on to the left (LH thread), followed by the keyed lock washer and the locknut. Adjust for optimal operation: running smoothly without play.

4. Install the pedal and the chain.

Thompson Bottom Bracket

Chances are you'll never see one of these. It is the standard on simple northern European (especially German) bicycles and as such sometimes found in Britain, but very rarely on the American continent. The illustration shows how it's put together. Assembly and disassembly is started from the LH side. The locknut has LH thread and must be loosened (to the right) before adjusting.

Adjusting (or removing and installing) the adjustable cone is done by turning the keyed dustcap, which has teeth that engage in slots in the

Left: The chainrings are attached to the spider on the RH crank with these bolts.

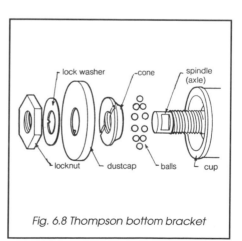

Fig. 6.8 Thompson bottom bracket

adjustable cone. All very clever and very simple once you know the trick. The bearing cups are press-fit into the bottom bracket shell — removal and installation as for one-piece cranks.

Chainring Maintenance

On a derailleur bike, the chainrings are installed on the RH crank by one of several methods. Once a month, ascertain that the chainrings are still firmly in place by tightening the little bolts that hold them to each other and to the cranks, respectively.

Most chainrings are attached with 5 mm Allen bolts, though some models use slotted nuts on one side, for which a slotted screwdriver or hooked tool is used.

Worn chainrings will result in increased resistance and poor shifting. Replace them if they are obviously worn or when teeth are cracked.

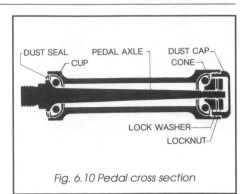

Fig. 6.10 Pedal cross section

If individual teeth are bent, they can sometimes be straightened. When the whole chainring is warped, it can be straightened by carefully using a wedge-shaped block of wood and pushing it between chainstay and chainring or between individual chainrings in the location where they are too close. These jobs can both be done while leaving the chainrings on the bike.

Replace Chainring

This job will be necessary when the chainrings are beyond repair or when you want to change to a different gearing range. First remove the crank, then undo the Allen bolts. The chainrings should not be reversed — remember to replace them facing the right direction. Shimano Superglide and off-round chainrings, such as the now virtually extinct Bio-Pace, have a marker that should be lined up with the crank arm for the correct orientation.

The Pedals

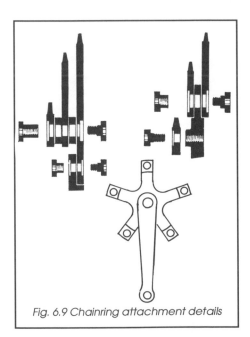

Fig. 6.9 Chainring attachment details

Pedals are screwed into the cranks with a normal RH threaded connection on the right, a LH one on the left. They are usually marked R and

L, but if you are not certain which pedal goes in which crank arm, do check the threading first.

Pedal maintenance operations are limited to adjustment, overhauling and the replacement of a pedal. There are various kinds of toe-clips for installation on the pedals, as well as clipless pedals which are becoming increasingly popular.

Replace Pedal

This job may also be necessary when transporting the bike on a plane or a bus. The description is equally valid for regular and clipless pedals.

Tools and equipment:
- 6 mm Allen key or pedal wrench
- *anti seize* lubricant or grease

Removal procedure:

1. Restrain the crank firmly by strad-dling the bicycle and placing your foot on either pedal. Place the pedal wrench around the pedal spindle and unscrew the RH pedal counterclockwise, the LH pedal clockwise. Once one pedal is removed, restrain that crank arm as you remove the other pedal.

2. Unscrew the connection between the pedal and the crank. If the pedal has a hexagonal recess in the end of the threaded stub (reached from behind the crank), you may attempt to use the Allen key. If the pedal is tight, the Allen key may not give sufficient leverage, even if there is a hexagonal recess.

Installation procedure:

1. Clean the threaded hole in the crank and the threaded stub on the pedal, then put some anti-seize or grease on both threaded parts.

2. Carefully align the screw thread and gently screw in the pedal by

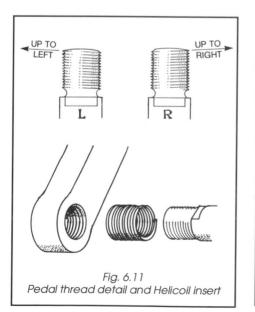

Fig. 6.11
Pedal thread detail and Helicoil insert

Use a special tool or a crescent wrench to straighten a bent chainring.

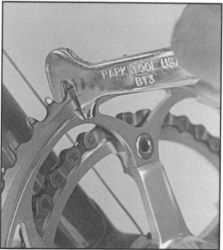

hand, turning the RH pedal clockwise, the LH pedal counterclockwise.

Notes:

1. If you remove the pedals frequently, place a 1–2 mm thin steel washer (again with some grease) between the face of the pedal stub and the face of the crank.

2. When the pedal hole in the crank is worn out, it can be drilled out and a Helicoil insert installed, which provides new screw thread.

Adjust Pedal Bearings

This description applies only to a djustable-bearing pedals. Cartridge pedals have sealed cartridge bearings that cannot be adjusted but must be replaced at a bike shop when they develop play or resistance.

Tools and equipment:
• 8–10 mm socket wrench
• small screwdriver
• dustcap tool, needle nose pliers, or 4–6 mm Allen key
• grease
• rag

Procedure:

1. Remove the dustcap.

2. Loosen the locknut by one turn.

3. Lift the underlying keyed washer with the tip of the screwdriver to loosen it.

4. Using the screwdriver, turn the cone one quarter turn to the right (clockwise) to tighten the bearing, to the left (counterclockwise) to loosen it.

5. Restraining the cone with the screwdriver to make sure it does not turn, tighten the locknut. Add grease if the bearings are dry.

6. Check and readjust if necessary. There should be neither noticeable play nor tightness.

7. Reinstall the dustcap.

Overhaul Pedal

This is required on an adjustable pedal if adjustment does not have the desired effect. Often the problem will be a bent spindle, and then — depending whether such parts are stocked for the model in question—you may have to replace the pedals.

As for cartridge-bearing pedals, to lubricate or replace their bearings, remove the bearing cartridges with the manufacturer's special tool; then pack the cartridge bearings with grease or replace them. If you have difficulty pushing them in, take them to a bike shop to have it done.

Hold back the crank while installing or removing a pedal.

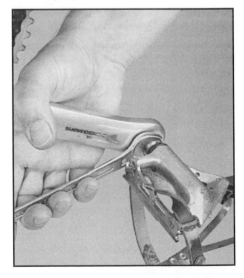

Tools and equipment:

- dustcap tool
- 8–10 mm socket wrench
- small screwdriver
- grease
- rag

Dismantling procedure:

1. Remove the dustcap, preferably using the special tool.

2. Loosen the locknut and remove it.

3. Lift the underlying keyed washer with the tip of the screwdriver to loosen it and then remove it.

4. Using the screwdriver, turn the cone to the left (counterclockwise) to loosen and remove it, catching the bearing balls with the rag placed underneath the pedal as you do so.

5. Pull the pedal housing off the spindle, also catching the bearing balls on the other side. Count and save all bearing balls. They are quite small and can be easily lost.

Overhauling procedure:

1. Clean and inspect all bearing surfaces and the pedal axle.

2. Replace anything that is damaged, corroded, grooved or pitted, as well as the pedal spindle if it is bent — or the whole pedal if no spares are available.

3. To make sure you get the right parts when replacing pedal parts or bearing balls, take the old ones to the bike shop for comparison.

Right: On conventional pedals, the bearings can be adjusted and overhauled.

Reassembly procedure:

1. Fill both bearing cups with grease and push the bearing balls in this bed of grease, making sure there is just a little room between — one less than the maximum that might seem to go in at a pinch.

2. Put the pedal housing on the spindle with the larger side (the end without the dustcap screw threading) first — towards the crank.

3. After you've made sure you have not lost any bearing balls, install the adjustable cone.

4. Install the keyed washer with the key fitting in the groove in the pedal spindle.

5. Install the locknut, while restraining the cone so it does not turn with it.

6. Adjust the bearing as described above.

7. Install the dustcap.

Clipless Pedals

In recent years, clipless pedals have become increasingly popular and are now available both for road bikes and for mountain bikes. They invariably run on cartridge bearings. The most important maintenance operation is exterior cleaning with water and a fine brush. The clipless pedal can be replaced following the same instructions that apply to ordinary pedals. To lubricate or replace the bearings, first remove the bearing cartridge with the manufacturer's special tool. Pack the cartridge bearings with grease.

The Chain

All derailleur bikes, whether meant for road use or off-road, are equipped with a narrow 3/32× 1/2 in. chain without a special connecting clip link. Single speeds and hub-geared bikes traditionally use the wider 1/8×1/2 in. chain with a connector clip link, often referred to as a master link (although recently the manufacturers

have started equipping them with narrower sprockets and chainrings that can be used wit the narrow chain). The life expectancy of a chain under off-road conditions is limited to about six months — even less if you ride a lot in mud, sand and dirt.

Clean and lubricate the chain as described in the section *Preventive Maintenance* in Chapter 3, depending on the kind of weather and terrain you ride in. From time to time, remove the chain to rinse it out in a solvent with 5–10% motor oil mixed in, and then lubricate it thoroughly. In the following section, we shall cover removal and installation of the chain.

Sometimes, when shifting problems occur after the bike has been in a spill, the reason will be a twisted chain. This may happen when the derailleur was twisted, trapping the chain in place. Check for this and replace the chain if it is twisted.

Many modern road bike pedals are disassembled from the crank side, including all clipless models.

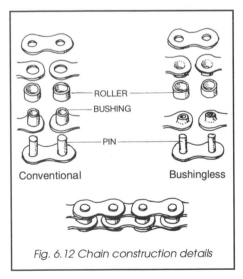

Fig. 6.12 Chain construction details

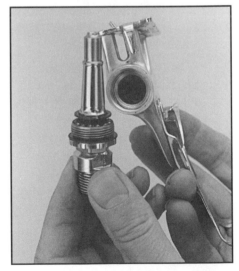

When selecting a new chain, make sure you get one that is particularly narrow if your bike has seven or eight cogs in the back. I find that set-ups with Shimano Hyperglide freewheel and Superglide chainrings work just as well with other narrow chains as with the special Hyperglide chain.

Replace Chain

This has to be done whenever you replace it or remove it for a thorough cleaning job. Also some derailleur maintenance operations are best done with the chain removed from the bike. The Shimano Hyperglide chain, which is designed to match the same company's special tooth shape on the chainrings and cogs, requires special attention. That will be covered in a note at the end of the description.

Tools and equipment:
- chain rivet extractor
- rags

Removal procedure:

1. With the aid of the derailleurs, and while turning the cranks with the rear wheel lifted off the ground, put the chain on the smallest chainring in the front and one of the smallest cogs at the back.

2. Put the chain rivet extractor on one of the pins between two links with the punch firmly up against the chain link pin. Retract the handle of the chain rivet extractor and place the chain in the slot farthest from the handle.

3. Turn in the handle by 6 turns, pushing the pin towards the opposite side.

4. Turn the handle back until the tool can be removed.

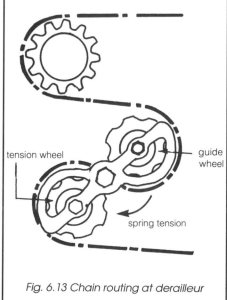

Fig. 6.13 Chain routing at derailleur

tension wheel

guide wheel

spring tension

Use the chain tool to disconnect or join the chain.

5. Try to separate the chain at this point, twisting it sideways. If that does not work, reinstall the tool and give it another turn until the chain comes apart. Make sure the pin does not come out altogether – if it does, replace the set of inner and outer links at the end.

Installation procedure:

1. Make sure the derailleurs are set for the smallest chainring in the front and the second smallest or smallest cog at the back.

2. Wrap the chain around the chainring, cog and derailleur, also passing through the front derailleur cage.

3. Routed this way, there should be just a little spring tension in the rear derailleur, tending to pull the chain tighter.

4. If the chain is too long, remove the links in sets of two — the outside link and the link within. Save these for spares.

5. Using the chain rivet extractor from the side where the pin

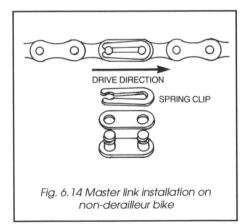

Fig. 6.14 Master link installation on non-derailleur bike

protrudes, push it back in until it projects equally on both sides.

6. Twist the chain sideways a few times until it has come loose enough at this point to bend as freely as at the other links. If this can't be done, put the tool on the chain in the other slot closest to the handle and turn the handle against the pin just a little until the links are freed.

General note:

If you should accidentally push the pin out all the way when disassembling, install a section of two new links instead, after removing two more links — taking care not to lose the pin this time. Use a section of the same make and type of chain.

Hyperglide note

The Shimano Hyperglide chain has one slightly oversize chain link pin that can be recognized because the link is black, and the chain should not be separated there. Instead split it anywhere else, and remove the pin all the way, then replace it with a special, longer, black pin that is available with the chain or as a replacement. Remove the end of this pin with pliers and file off the pointed end of this special link before trying out the gears.

Master link note:

To replace the wider chain used on bikes without derailleur gearing, make sure the clip on the master link, which is used to connect the two ends, is installed in the correct direction (the closed end should travel forward). The spring clip is lifted off

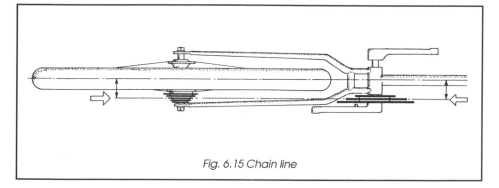

Fig. 6.15 Chain line

with a screwdriver and it is prized off and put back on. Adjust the chain length and tension so that it can be moved up or down by a total of 2 cm (¾ in.). If necessary, fine-tune by installing the wheel farther to the back or the front in the drop-outs.

Chain Line

Ideally, the chain should run parallel to a line through the center of the bike's frame and wheels. On derailleur bikes this means that the point in the middle of the chainrings should be in line with the middle of the freewheel block. On non-derailleur bikes, the chainring should be in line with the cog. To achieve that, it may be possible to adjust the bottom bracket cups sideways on a derailleur bike. Use a different shaped cog on a bike without derailleurs. Sometimes a parallel line can only be achieved by straightening the frame (if the problem is due to misalignment).

The Freewheel

Most manufacturers use a freewheel block with six or seven cogs (also called sprockets) that is screwed on the screw thread of the rear hub. However, the cassette-hubs, such as the Shimano Freehub, are becoming quite popular. On these models, the freewheel mechanism is integrated in a cassette attached to the rear hub with a large internal hollow Allen

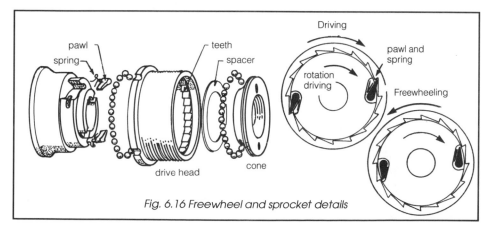

Fig. 6.16 Freewheel and sprocket details

bolt, while the cogs are installed on splines and locked in place by means of a threaded ring or a threaded smallest cog. As far as the guts of a freewheel mechanism are concerned, I shall not go into any detail here. If the freewheel doesn't work, get a new one (or a new freewheel cassette, in the case of the cassette hub). What is more important is knowing how to lubricate the mechanism, how to exchange cogs and how to remove a complete freewheel block or cassette. Those are the subjects that will be covered here.

Freewheel Block Lubrication

Do this job if the freewheel block is running roughly, yet is not so old that it seems reasonable to replace it — I suggest once a year. For cassette type freewheels, first remove the wheel axle and wheel bearings, starting from the RH side, then use a special tool called Freehub-Buddy that is

screwed into the end of the cassette body to squirt in the lubricant.

Tools and equipment:
- SAE 40 or thicker oil
- old can or similar receptacle
- brush
- rag

Procedure:

1. Before you lubricate the mechanism, clean the cogs, the spaces between them and the visible end of the freewheel block, preferably with the wheel removed from the bike. This can be done using an old rag or stiff brush.

2. On freewheel blocks with an oil hole, add oil until it oozes out at the other end.

3. On freewheel blocks without an oil hole, put the wheel on its side with the freewheel block facing up, and a receptacle under the

Left: Removing a conventional screwed-on freewheel with a matching freewheel removal tool.

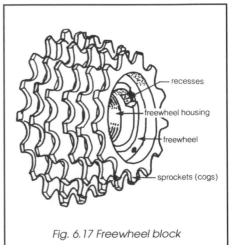

Fig. 6.17 Freewheel block

hub to catch excess oil. Turn the hub relative to the wheel, and introduce oil into the gap that is visible between stationary and turning parts of the freewheel block mechanism — until it comes out clean on the other side.

4.   Let it drip until no more oil comes out, then clean off excess oil.

Replace Screwed-on Freewheel Block

Once the wheel is removed from the bicycle, you can usually tell a freewheel block from a freewheel cassette, because on these models there will be internal splines or notches into which a freewheel tool fits.

Tools and equipment:
• freewheel tool
• wrench or vise
• 10-inch crescent wrench
• grease

Removal procedure:

1.   Remove the rear wheel from the bike.

2.   Remove the quick-release or the axle nut and its washer on the RH side.

3.   Place the freewheel tool on the freewheel block with the ribs or prongs on the tool exactly matching the splines or notches in the freewheel body.

4.   Install the quick-release or the RH axle nut, leaving 2 mm (3/32 in.) space .

5.   If you have a vise available, clamp the tool in with the side matching **the freewheel** facing up; if not,

place the wrench on the flat faces of the tool and clamp the wheel securely, with the tire pushed against the floor and one wall of the room. Be careful when using SunTour removers to avoid breaking off their fragile prongs.

6.   Turning counterclockwise to loosen the screw thread between hub and freewheel, forcefully turn either the wheel relative to the vise, or the wrench relative to the wheel — about one turn, until the space between the tool and the nut is taken up.

7.   Loosen the nut another two turns and repeat this process until the freewheel can be removed by hand, holding the tool.

Installation procedure:

1.   Clean the threaded surfaces of the freewheel block (inside) and the hub (outside), and coat these

Cassette freewheels are held onto the special matching hub with a hollow Allen bolt.

surfaces with grease to prevent corrosion and to ease subsequent removal.

2. Put the wheel down horizontally with the threaded end facing up.

3. Carefully screw the freewheel block on by hand, making sure that it is correctly threaded on, until it cannot be tightened further that way.

4. Install the wheel, and allow the driving force to tighten it as you ride.

Replace Cassette Freewheel

If no internal notches or splines to take a tool are visible, you probably have a cassette type freewheel. It is held inside the rear hub with an internal Allen bolt.

Tools and equipment:
• 9 or 10 mm Allen key

Removal procedure:

1. Dismantle the hub bearing on the LH side, and remove the axle.

2. Hold the wheel firmly and un-screw the freewheel cassette (with

its cogs) with the big Allen key (10 mm for Shimano, 9 mm for Sun-Tour and Campagnolo).

Installation procedure:

1. Carefully clean and very lightly lubricate the thread of the freewheel cassette and the hole in the hub.

2. Accurately place the freewheel cassette (with its cogs) in the hub.

3. Tighten the freewheel cassette with the big Allen key.

Note:

If the wheel locks up, it is probably because the internal Allen bolt is not tightened down fully. To correct this problem, remove the RH locknut and cone, then pull the axle from the LH side and tighten the freewheel cassette with the 9 or 10 mm Allen key. Then reassemble.

Replace Sprocket on Cassette Freewheel

On these units, the cogs are held in splines on the freewheel cassette, held together with a lockring

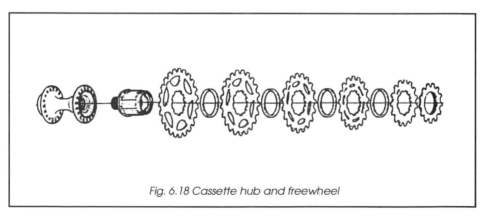

Fig. 6.18 Cassette hub and freewheel

(Shimano) or a screwed-on smallest cog (SunTour and Campagnolo).

On Shimano Hyperglide cogs, which owe their easy shifting to subtle alignment of specially shaped teeth, one of the splines is wider, so make sure you line them up properly.

Tools and equipment:
• 2 chain whips
• freewheel tool (for Shimano Hyperglide mountain bike models)
• 10-inch crescent wrench

Dismantling procedure:

1. Remove the wheel from the bike.

2. Place the wheel horizontally in front of you with the freewheel cassette facing up.

3. On Shimano Hyperglide models, use the chain whip to restrain the largest cog while using the freewheel tool to unscrew the locking cog. Other freewheel cassettes can be removed with two chain whips by simply turning the last (smallest) cog against the biggest one.

4. Remove the cogs and the spacers, noting the sequence of the various cogs and spacers.

Installation procedure:

1. Install the cogs and the spacers in the same sequence.

2. Screw on the last cog or the notched ring, while countering with a chain whip wrapped around one of the other cogs (on road models).

Right: Use of chain whips to replace freewheel sprockets on a cassette type

3. Use the freewheel tool to install the lockring on Shimano Hyperglide models.

Note on Shimano XTR:

On these lightweight cassette freewheel hubs the larger cogs are installed on a stepped spider and are held with three long bolts. To replace them, unscrew the lockring using the freewheel tool, and remove the smaller cogs first.

Replace Sprocket on Screwed-on Freewheel Block

On these conventional units, most or all of the cogs are screwed onto the freewheel. The procedure is similar to that outlined for the cassette freewheel, except that you will always need two chain whips, one wrapped around the smallest cog, one around one of the other ones. When you have finished reassembly,

put the chain on the smallest cog and stand on the pedals to tighten it. Readjust the derailleur, if necessary.

Minor Freewheel Overhaul

Do this work to eliminate the wobbling effect of an obviously loose freewheel mechanism. In addition, it may be worthwhile in other cases of freewheel trouble, since you may solve the problem without having to replace the freewheel. First remove the rear wheel from the bike, but leave the freewheel on the hub. Clean the outside of the freewheel (also between the cogs) before commencing. Although the description assumes a conventional screwed-on freewheel, the same work can be done on a cassette type freewheel. In that case, first remove the wheel axle by undoing the LH side bearing.

Tools and equipment:
• special pin wrench (or a drift and a hammer
• rag
• bearing grease
• 30–45 cm (12–15 in.) piece of twine

Procedure

1. Using hammer and drift (or special fitting pin wrench) unscrew the part shown in the illustration; this is actually the freewheel bearing cone and has LH screw thread; unscrew it by turning to the right.

Fig. 6.19
Freewheel mechanism overhaul

2. Remove the shim (or one of several shims) that is installed under the cone. This reduces the gap between the two bearing races and usually solves the problem.

Note:

If you had another problem, proceed disassembling the mechanism to establish whether it can be corrected. Embed the bearing balls in a generous layer of bearing grease. Fig. 6.19 shows how to hold the mechanism together so it can be reinserted in the freewheel housing.

3. Reinstall the freewheel bearing cone by screwing to the left, tightening firmly; then check whether it is operating smoothly now. If necessary, remove another shim or replace it with one of another thickness.

CHAPTER 7

Derailleur Gearing

Nowadays, most adult bikes are equipped with derailleur gears, although hub gearing is still used on some bikes and will be covered in Chapter 8. The derailleur system comprises a front derailleur, also called changer, and a rear derailleur, sometimes referred to as a mechanism outside the U.S.

Both are operated by means of shift levers that are mounted either on the handlebars or on the downtube. The shifters are connected to the derailleurs by means of flexible Bowden cables. The rear derailleur moves the chain sideways from one sprocket, or cog, to another on the rear wheel mounted freewheel block, while the front derailleur moves the chain sideways from one chainring to another.

Derailleur System Overview

Since the various cogs and chainrings have different numbers of teeth, varying the combination achieves a lower or higher gear. A low gear is achieved by selecting a small chainring in the front and a big cog in the rear. A high gear results when a large chainring is combined with a small cog.

Essentially all derailleur bikes sold since 1986 come equipped with indexed gearing. That means that there are distinct stops on the shift levers for each of the gears, eliminating the need for sensitive adjustments when shifting. For mountain bike use, there are two major types of shift levers, mounted on top of and under the handlebars respectively. Hybrids and touring bikes with drop handlebars are often equipped with bar-end shifters.

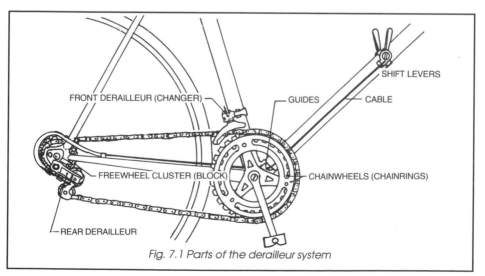

Fig. 7.1 Parts of the derailleur system

For road bikes, several manufacturers have introduced gear shifters integrated in the brake levers. By and large, these systems are maintained and adjusted just like any other indexed derailleur system. The integrated brake-and-gear-levers are one unit, so you'll have to replace the entire lever unit if either the brake lever or the gear shifter is damaged beyond repair.

This chapter will describe all maintenance operations necessary to maintain and adjust the gearing system and its individual components. I advise purchasing a shifter that is made by the same manufacturer as the derailleur, which in turn will work best on a matching freewheel.

Adjust Derailleur Range

The most frequently occurring derailleur problem requiring maintenance is that one of the derailleurs either exceeds its full range or fails to reach it. Another common problem is when

indexed shifting doesn't work properly, and the chain gets stuck between the chainrings or cogs.

Tools and equipment:
small screwdriver
rag

Procedure:

1. Establish what the nature of your problem is:
   ☐ front or rear derailleur
   ☐ too far or not far enough
   ☐ left or right

2. If necessary, put the chain back on the chainring or the cog, operating the shift lever to position the derailleur if necessary.

3. Observe how each derailleur is equipped with two set-stop screws, usually equipped with a little spring under the head, and usually marked with an H and an L for high and low gear, respectively.

Front derailleur mounted on seat-tube lug.

Modern rear derailleur.

4. Tightening one of these screws limits the range of the derailleur in the appropriate direction, while loosening the screw extends it.

5. If the chain came off on the RH side (outside, or high gear) on the front, tighten the screw marked H of the front derailleur by perhaps one turn. If it did not quite reach the last gear on that side, loosen the screw by about that much.

6. Check all the gears, turning the cranks with the rear wheel lifted off the ground. Readjust as necessary.

Note:

If problems persist, adjust the relevant derailleur system completely, as described for front and rear derailleurs separately below.

The Rear Derailleur

Indexed mechanisms are almost always used on modern bikes, and generally set up to select one of 6, 7 or 8 cogs (only 5 on older models). The RH shifter has a ratchet device that corresponds with specific settings of the rear derailleur, which in turn correspond with the positions of the individual cogs.

In the case of downtube and over-the-bar shifters, there is usually a small selection lever to switch from the indexed mode to the so-called friction mode (actually just a finer ratchet), which allows the selection of intermediate positions. This is essential when the mechanism is no longer adjusted properly, allowing the selection of the right gear, especially for people who are not familiar with making derailleur adjustments. On or off-road, this will be your quick solution to any gearing

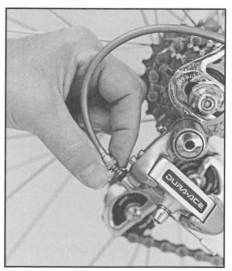

Left: Adjusting the range of a rear derailleur.
Below: Adjusting cable tension.

problems that develop, since exact adjustment is more easily carried out at home. The index and friction modes are usually identified by the letters I and F, respectively, marked on the shifter.

Adjust Rear Derailleur

Most gearing problems can be eliminated by some form of derailleur adjustment.

Tools and equipment:
- small screwdriver
- 5 mm Allen key
- 8 mm wrench

Procedure:

1. To get by until you have time to do a more thorough adjusting job, select the friction mode on the RH shifter if you have downtube or over-the-bar shifters.

2. Adjust the cable tension, using the built-in adjusting barrel.

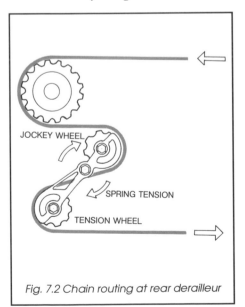

Fig. 7.2 Chain routing at rear derailleur

3. Shift the rear derailleur to the highest gear (smallest cog) while holding the bike's rear wheel off the ground. Shift the front derailleur to the largest chainring. Use your hand to turn the cranks to engage the chain in that gear (or the closest one to it).

4. Tighten or loosen the barrel to either release or increase tension on the cable. If the cable is too loose, you will notice this now.

5. If the range of the adjusting barrel is inadequate, the cable must be clamped in at a different point. Screw the adjusting barrel in all the way, loosen the eye bolt or clamp nut that holds the cable at the derailleur, pull the cable from the end until it is taut but not under tension, and tighten the clamp nut or eye bolt again.

6. Try out all the gears and readjust the range if necessary, following the description above.

7. Now the derailleur operates correctly in friction mode. The next step will be to fine-tune the indexing. To do that, first with the shifter still set in the friction mode, select the lowest gear (biggest cog in the rear, combined with smallest chainring in the front) and make sure it achieves this gear correctly.

8. Select the highest gear again (largest chainring, smallest cog), then put the shifter in index mode, marked with the letter I.

9. Adjust the cable tension until the chain runs smoothly without scraping against the derailleur cage or the next larger cog.

10. Move the shifter one notch for the next lower gear in the back, engaging the second smallest cog if it is adjusted correctly.

11. If the derailleur does not move the chain to the next cog, tighten the cable by about one half revolution of the adjusting barrel.

12. If the derailleur shifts past this second smallest cog, loosen the cable tension with the adjusting barrel by about half a turn.

13. Repeat steps 10 through 12 until the mechanism works smoothly in these two gears.

14. With the derailleur set for the second smallest cog, tighten the cable with the adjusting barrel just so far that the chain runs noisily, scraping against the third smallest cog.

15. Loosen the cable tension just so far that the noises are subdued, to achieve the optimal setting.

16. Ride the bicycle and attempt to shift all gears to verify correct adjustments.

Notes:
☐ If adjusting does not solve the problem, first replace the cable and outer cable. Sometimes simply filing the newly cut outer cable end will solve your problems.

☐ Most rear derailleurs have a third adjusting screw, with which the angle of the mechanism can be varied. Select the gear in which the chain runs on the biggest cog, and adjust it so that the chain comes close to it, without the cog scraping the pulley.

☐ Many new mountain bikes with under-the-bar shifters also have a cable adjustment that is located next to the shifter's ratchet. It should be tightened before attempting a rear cable adjustment.

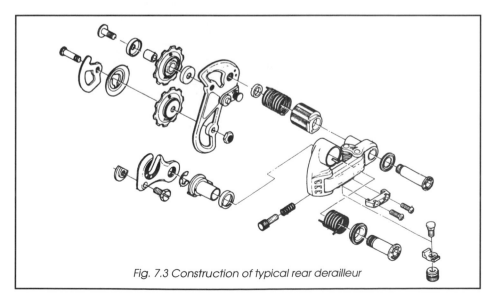

Fig. 7.3 Construction of typical rear derailleur

Overhaul Rear Derailleur

This work will be necessary when so much dirt has built up that operation of the mechanism has become un-reliable and cannot be solved by a djusting.

Tools and equipment:
- 3 mm Allen key
- 7 mm open-ended wrench
- 2 small crescent wrenches
- solvent
- rags
- grease and spray lubricant

Procedure:

1. Remove the bolts at the little wheels, called tension and jockey pulley respectively, over which the chain runs, catching the wheels, bushings and bolts.

2. Clean the wheels and the bushings inside, as well as all other parts of the mechanism that are more easily accessible now.

3. If the pulleys appear to be worn, take them to a bike shop and buy new ones. Although they look alike, they do differ — on many models the tension pulley even differs from the jockey pulley — so exact replacements are necessary.

4. If the cage is bent, carefully straighten it using two crescent wrenches — one on either side of the bend. Continue dismantling only if the mechanism cannot be cleaned adequately without doing so. Before removing the hinged cage, visualize how the internal spring works, so you will be able to reinstall it correctly. If necessary, you can increase the spring ten-

sion by placing the end in a different notch.

5. Lubricate the bushings in the pulleys with grease and all pivots with light spraycan oil.

6. Reassemble the chain cage with the pulley, guiding the chain through the cage.

7. Try out all the gears and adjust the derailleur if necessary.

Replace Rear Derailleur

This is done when you overhaul the bike completely and when the derailleur must be replaced because its operation cannot be restored by adjusting or replacing parts. Generally, a short-cage derailleur can be used, whatever was used originally, providing the largest rear cog does not exceed 28 teeth. These models work more predictably and are less fragile than the long-cage version.

Installing rear derailleur.

Tools and equipment:
- chain rivet extractor
- 5 mm Allen key
- small screwdriver
- rag
- grease

Removal procedure:

1. If you prefer to leave the chain intact, open up the cage by removing the bolt of the jockey pulley.

2. Otherwise, separate the chain using the chain rivet tool.

3. Cut the cable crimp, undo the cable attachment and catch the ferrules and cable housing.

4. Undo the derailleur attachment bolt and remove the derailleur.

Installation procedure:

1. When buying a new derailleur, make sure that it is compatible with the shifter and the freewheel block installed on the bike. For example, if you have a 7- or 8-speed shifter, you need a derailleur with enough travel for that distance.

2. Clean and grease the derailleur eye threads, and gently screw in the derailleur. Put the new derailleur in the same position as the old one was, checking to make sure it pivots freely around the mounting bolt.

3. Attach the cable.

4. Either install the chain (if it had been removed) or open up the cage by removing the bolt of the jockey pulley to put the chain in place, then reinstall the guide wheel.

5. Try out all the gears and adjust the derailleur and the cable tension if necessary.

The Front Derailleur

Although many mountain bike front derailleurs, or changers, are also indexed, requiring a matching indexed shifter, road bikes are usually equipped with non-indexed models, because there are only 2 chainrings to choose from.

The major maintenance work on the front derailleur is the range ad-

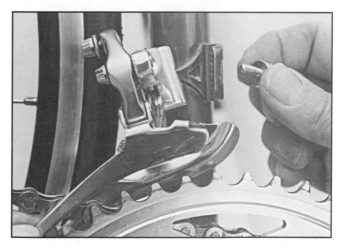

Installing front derailleur, showing mounting height relative to chainrings and adjusting screws.

justing procedure described above. In addition, the cable tension can be adjusted similarly to that for the rear derailleur when it does not shift properly. Most front derailleurs used for road bikes do not have a cable adjuster built into the outer cable. In that case, any adjustments have to be made by repositioning the clamp on the inner cable.

Adjust Front Derailleur

This job must be done when the front derailleur "dumps" the chain by the side of the chainrings or when one chainring cannot be reached, or when the chain scrapes on the derailleur cage.

Tools and equipment:
5 and 6 mm Allen keys
small screwdriver

Procedure:

1. First make sure the derailleur cage if perfectly parallel to the chainring — loosen the attachment bolt and twist the derailleur into position before retightening if necessary.

2 Carry out any adjustment of the set-stop screws that may be necessary.

3. Set the shifter in the position for the highest gear with the chain on the large outside chainring.

4. In this position, the cable should be just taut, though not under tension.

5. If necessary, tension or loosen it by clamping the cable in at a different point: loosen the eye bolt or clamp

Right: Opening up the front derailleur cage (not possible on all models).

nut with either the 5 mm Allen key or 8 mm wrench, pull the cable taut and tighten the eye bolt or clamp nut again.

6. Check all gears and make any other adjustments that may be necessary.

Replace Front Derailleur

This may become necessary if the mechanism is bent or damaged — usually the result of a fall.

Tools and equipment:
5 or 6 mm Allen key
small screwdriver
chain rivet extractor

Removal procedure:

1. Loosen the cable attachment by unscrewing the eye bolt or the clamp nut, and pull the cable end out.

2. Either remove the chain with the chain rivet extractor or, on some

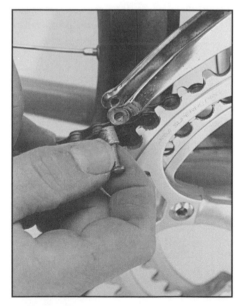

models, you can open up the derailleur's chain guide cage by removing the little bolt through the bushing that connects the two sides in the back of the cage.

3. Undo the attachment bolt.

Installation procedure:

1. Install the derailleur on the seat tube, with the cage parallel to the chainrings. Don't tighten it solidly yet.

2. Fine-tune the position, leaving a distance of 2–4 mm (3/32–3/16 in.) clearance between the largest chainring and the bottom of the cage, making sure it is aligned. Now tighten the attachment bolt fully.

3. Feed the cable through the mechanism as shown, and attach it in the eye bolt or under the clamp nut.

4. Adjust the cable tension so that it is just taut, but not under tension, with the shifter set for the highest gear and the chain on the largest chainring.

5. Check all the gears and adjust the derailleur range if necessary.

The Shifters

Whatever the shifter type, if it does not give satisfactory service, as evidenced by the derailleur's jumping out of the selected gear, the reason may be a damaged or corroded derailleur cable. So first check it, and replace cable and outer cable if necessary.

If the cable and the derailleur themselves are working properly, the

problem may be due to either insufficient tension on the spring inside the mechanism, dirt or corrosion, or wear of the notched ring inside. Only in the latter case will it be necessary to replace the shifter.

First try cleaning and tensioning the shifter. Do not attempt to take your shifter apart unless it is a friction shifter. If it is, you can take it apart carefully and note where the various bits and pieces go. Then clean and lightly lubricate all parts with grease. Finally reassemble and if necessary turn the screw that holds it all together a little tighter.

Replace Shifter

If the shifter cannot be made to work by means of adjustment and cable replacement, it can easily be replaced.

Replacing or overhauling the rear derailleur's pulleys. On some models, the two pulleys should not be interchanged.

Tools and equipment:
- 5 mm Allen key
- small screwdriver
- 8 mm wrench

Removal procedure:

1. Undo the inner cable clamp at the derailleur.

2. Remove the shifter attachment screw.

3. Pull the inner cable out and catch the cable casing and any loose items.

Installation procedure:

1. Attach the shifter in the desired location.

2. Feed the cable through the shifter with the nipple in the recess.

3. Guide the cable through the various guides and the cable casing, and attach the end at the derailleur.

Clamping in the end of the front derailleur cable, while pulling it taut.

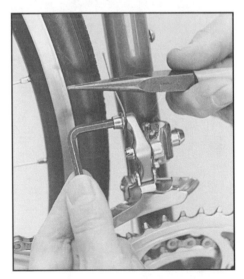

4. Adjust the derailleur cable tension as described separately for front and rear derailleurs above.

Note:

In the Shimano STI and Campagnolo Ergopower systems, the shifters are combined with the brake levers. They are installed, removed and replaced together with the brake levers and you can follow the instruction for bar-end shifters.

Replace Bar-End Shifters

This type of shift lever requires special attention when installing, and the same procedure can be followed for SIS and other units with integrated shifting and braking controls. There are two basic types: with the cable routed through the handlebars or the cable routed outside the handlebars. The former require holes drilled in the handlebars, for which reason (or rather the resulting loss of strength) I would advise you to steer clear of them. If your handlebars have the holes pre-drilled, you may use that type, but I'd certainly advise you to get a model for external cable routing, rather than drill your own holes.

Tools and equipment:
- wrenches to fit cable clamp bolt at derailleur and locknut on lever pivot bolt
- pliers
- medium screwdriver
- Allen key for internal mounting bolt
- lubricant

Disassembly procedure:

1. Place bike in the gear corresponding to the normal position for both derailleurs (always small cog in the rear, usually small chainwheel in the front).

2. Loosen the cable at the derailleur and free it from the guides and sections of inner cable as far as possible.

3. Unscrew the lever pivot bolt and remove the bushing and the locknut on the other side.

4. Remove the lever with the two washers, then remove the inner cable.

5. With the Allen key, loosen the internal mounting bolt, turning to the right; this will loosen the expander plug that holds the lever assembly mounting body in the end of the handlebars.

6. Now remove the inner cable (if run through the handlebars); remove the handlebar tape and outer cable in case you want to replace it and it is run outside the handlebars.

Installation procedure:

1. If the cable is to be run outside the handlebars, old handlebar tape and the old outer cable may have to be removed first.

2. Check to make sure the chain is in the gear that corresponds to the normal position for both derailleurs (small cog in the rear, usually small chainwheel in the front).

3. Route the outer cable along the handlebar the way it interferes least, but always at the bottom near the end where the lever is to be installed; attach with short pieces of adhesive tape (or run the cables through the handlebars if these have holes).

4. Wrap handlebar tape around the handlebars, as outlined in Chapter 11.

5. Loosely assemble the control body without the lever (i.e. expander plug, mounting bolt and mounting body), with the slot for the lever in line with the outer cable facing down. Tighten the mounting bolt by turning it to the left with the Allen key.

6. Slightly lubricate the lever bushing and contact surfaces, then install the lever, placing washers on either side. Tighten the pivot screw and the locknut.

7. Lubricate the cable, then thread the cable through the lever in such a way that the nipple will lie in the recess in the lever; now push the cable through the outer cable, over

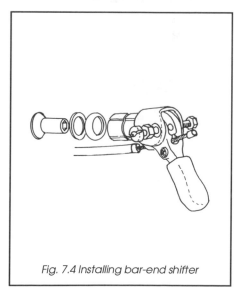

Fig. 7.4 Installing bar-end shifter

the guides, and attach to the derailleur. Alternately, you may prefer to thread the inner cable
through the lever and the outer
cable before installing the lever in
the mounting unit — it always
must be done this way when the
cable is run through the handlebars.

8. Place the lever in the horizontal
   position and pull the cable taut
   with the pliers at the derailleur,
   then attach firmly. Make any adjustments as described for the
   front and rear derailleurs elsewhere in this chapter.

Twistgrip Shifter

These devices are mainly used on
some entry-level mountain bikes and
hybrids. However, they are suitable
for retrofitting as a replacement for
conventional shifters. The GripShift
works with any Shimano or SunTour
derailleur, while the Campagnolo
and Sachs models only work well
with the same manufacturer's
derailleurs.

Procedure:

1. Follow the instructions for cable
   removal above, and then remove
   the old shifter and the handgrip.

2. Hook the cable nipple in the recess
   and route the cable through from
   inside, keeping the outer cable in
   place.

3. Install the twistgrip like any other
   handgrip, but tighten it with the
   clamping screw when it is in such
   a position that the numbers are
   visible from the rider's position.

4. Route the cable to the derailleur
   and clamp it in, keeping the outer
   cable taut.

5. Put the twistgrip shifter in the
   position for the highest gear and
   clamp in the end. Adjust the
   derailleur until the cable is taut.

6. Adjust the cable tension until all
   the gears work properly.

Derailleur Cables

For indexed shifters, relatively stiff
stainless steel inner cables and a
nylon sleeve between inner cable and

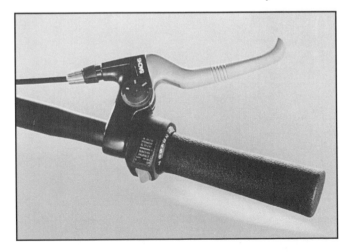

*Twist grip shifter used
on some derailleur
bikes. Especially
suitable for lower-end
mountain bikes and
hybrids.*

outer cable were introduced. These same cables can also be used on non-indexed systems. They only need to be cleaned from time to time and checked to make sure they are not pinched or damaged anywhere. Other cables (without the nylon sleeve) must also be lubricated from time to time. This is best done by removing them and smearing grease over the inner cable. Alternatively, squirt a few drops of oil between the inner cable and the cable casing at the ends where the inner cable disappears into the casing.

Replace Derailleur Cable

This work is necessary if the cable is pinched or otherwise damaged, or if the inner cable shows signs of corrosion or frayed strands. If you have under-the-bar shifters, the cable must match the shifter, since the two major

Replacing derailleur cable.

manufacturers (SunTour and Shimano) use different nipples.

Tools and equipment:
- 5 mm Allen key
- 8 mm wrench
- cable cutters
- screwdriver
- file

Removal procedure:

1. Undo the cable at the derailleur by loosening the cable clamp nut or the eye bolt that holds the cable to the derailleur.

2. Put the shifter in the position for the highest gear.

3. On under-the-bar shifters, open up the mechanism only to the point where the cable and the nipple are exposed.

Cutting the cable end. Especially the outer casing should only be cut to size if you have the proper tool.

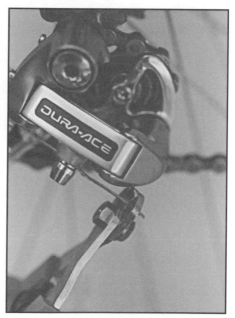

Soldering the end of a cable.

4. Push the cable free at the shifter.

5. Pull the cable out and catch the outer cable and any other loose items such as cable end caps and ferrules.

Installation procedure:

1. Grease the cable, and file the outer cable ends if it is a replacement.

2. Feed the cable through the shifter as shown, with the nipple in the recess. If there is a nipple at each end, cut off the one that you won't use.

3. Guide the inner cable through the various guides and stops on the frame and the cable casing, then thread it through the derailleur clamp. Apply gentle torque once correct tension is established.

4. After you have established the correct cable length and have adjusted the tension, crimp or solder the strands of the inner cable end together to prevent fraying.

CHAPTER 8

Hub Gearing

Although hub gearing is not much used on modern bicycles in the U.S., recent developments make this alternative gearing method a logical choice for many cyclists. Shimano, Sachs and Sturmey-Archer now each offer systems that promise a return of hub gearing on bicycles intended for practical use. In addition, there are still bicycles on the road that are equipped with earlier models, and I feel owners of those bikes are just as entitled to practical information as the rest of us with derailleur-geared bikes.

Today, hub gearing is available with anywhere from 2 to 7 gears. Generally, the more common 3-speed hubs are operated by means of a single handlebar-mounted shifter which pulls a little chain or hinge connected with the selector mechanism in the hub via a flexible cable that runs over rollers or guides. On most 5-speed models there are two cables and two selector mechanisms.

The hub axle is hollow and carries the selector rod on which the clutch mechanism is held. On most models, the selector rod is attached to a little chain, while other models connect it with a hinge mechanism screwed on in the location of the axle nut. The cable is attached to the little chain or the hinge by means of a cable adjuster which serves to correct the adjustment of the gears. When shifting towards a lower gear, the rod

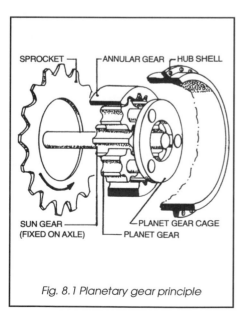

SPROCKET — ANNULAR GEAR — HUB SHELL

SUN GEAR (FIXED ON AXLE) — PLANET GEAR CAGE — PLANET GEAR

Fig. 8.1 Planetary gear principle

Modern hub gearing system from Sturmey-Archer with aluminum shell hubs and combined with drum brakes. Shifter options inlcude a single handlebar-mounted lever and dual stem-mounted levers. stem-mounted shifters.

is pulled further out and sets the selector in the appropriate position.

The two-speed gear, used mainly for portable bicycles, works without external controls: it is operated by pedaling backwards.

Hub Gear Maintenance

Whenever hub gearing does not work properly, it is generally not due to the mechanism itself, but rather to the controls. Slipped cable guides or pinched cables are the most frequent causes of control problems. Consequently, these points should be checked before attempting to adjust the mechanism.

Most models made by Sachs are lubricated for life and only break down when the hub overheats on models with built-in back-pedaling brake. In that case, the hub should be dismantled and the bearings repacked with the manufacturer's special grease. Most other models are equipped with an oil nipple and should be lubricated with 10 drops of light oil once every three months or whenever the hub appears not to run or shift smoothly.

On 3-speed models, the coaster brake can be eliminated by dismantling the unit and removing the sectioned, cylindrical brake mantle with the brake cone (for details, see Chapter 10).

To date, Sturmey-Archer's models with built-in drum brakes are not equipped with a seal that separates the brake from the gears. The result is that when the bike lies on its left side, the oil enters the brake drum where it ruins the brake shoes. Consequently, the manufacturer delivers them unlubricated — make sure you lubricate such a hub before use — and don't lay the bike on its LH side....

Adjust Sturmey-Archer 3-Speed Hub

On these hubs, the cable is connected to a tiny chain that comes out of the RH axle nut. The correct adjustment can be checked based on the alignment seen through a viewing port in this nut. Generally, no tools are required, although a pair of pliers may be needed if the adjuster is too tight.

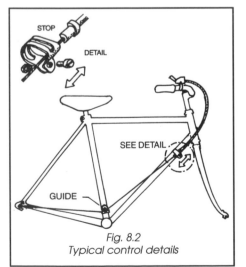

Fig. 8.2
Typical control details

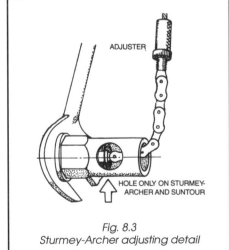

Fig. 8.3
Sturmey-Archer adjusting detail

Procedure:

1. Establish whether the cable and any rollers are in order, and the stops and guides are attached properly. Correct if necessary.

2. If the hub has not been lubricated for more than 3 months, first lubricate it through the oil hole, then turn the cranks several times in each gear with the wheel lifted off the ground.

3. Place the shift lever in the normal gear position (N or 2), while turning the cranks at least half a revolution.

4. Check the situation through the viewing port in the RH axle nut. The hub is correctly adjusted if the shoulder on the internal pin to which the chain is connected is exactly aligned with the end of the wheel axle (if necessary, move the shift lever back and forth a little to check).

5. If necessary, adjust the cable adjuster. To do this, loosen the lock-

To replace the cable or the shifter, pull the shifter down all the way and push the cable out.

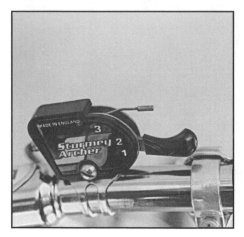

nut, turn the internally threaded bushing relative to the threaded pin, then hold in position while tightening the locknut.

6. Check and re-adjust if necessary.

Adjust Sachs 3-Speed Hub

Models made since about 1975 do not have a neutral position. Consequently, the problem here never shows as loss of transmission, but merely by the fact that a different gear from the one selected remains engaged. The adjustment is done in the high gear, and no tools are required.

Procedure:

1. Establish whether the cable, its guides and stops, and the shifter all operate correctly and the stops and guides are not loose. Correct if necessary.

Sachs uses a click box which is just pushed over the end of the controls at the hub and is supposed to be set for correct adjustment.

2. Place the shift lever in the high gear position (H or 3), while turning the cranks at least half a revolution.

3. Adjust the special cable adjuster, which is simply clamped on a serrated rod. Push the clip in, slide it up or down, holding the serrated rod in the other hand, until the cable is just taut but not under tension, and let go of the clip.

4. Check and re-adjust if necessary.

Adjust Shimano 3-Speed Hub

On these hubs, the controls are carried via a *bell crank*, or hinge mechanism on the LH side of the hub. This hinge mechanism has an integral locknut and must be positioned so that the pivoting movement is fully aligned with the cable. To achieve this, you may have to loosen the locknut a little, adjust the bell crank in the right position, and then hold it there while tightening the locknut. Generally, no tools will be required for the rest of the work.

Procedure:

1. Check whether the cable, its guides and stops, the bell crank, and the shifter all operate correctly and the stops, guides and bell crank are properly attached. Correct if necessary.

2. Place the shift lever in the high gear position (N or 2), while turning the cranks at least half a revolution.

3. If the gears are correctly adjusted, the letter N (or the number 2) should now be completely visible in the window in the bell crank.

4. If it is not, adjust the cable adjuster attached to the bell crank until the number is visible in the window.

5. Check each of the gears in turn, while turning the cranks with the wheel lifted, and re-adjust if necessary.

5-speed shift lever and cables. This is the Sachs model, but Sturmey-Archer's is quite similar.

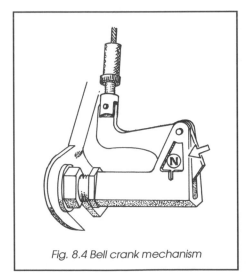

Fig. 8.4 Bell crank mechanism

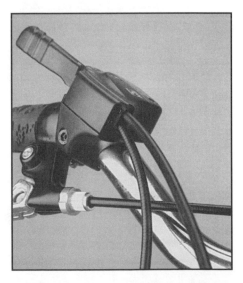

5-Speed Hubs

These units include a double set of planetary gears inside, each with its own controls. They are available from Sturmey-Archer and Sachs. The one made by Sturmey-Archer is available with and without built-in drum brake. Sachs makes versions without brake, with a cable-operated drum brake and with a coaster brake.

The more recent models are not operated by means of two separate shift levers, but by a single lever that controls the two cables. Although this may seem simpler to use, it is considerably more prone to trouble, and by no means easier to adjust. The main problem is that these shifters are made of a relatively soft fibre-reinforced plastic which deforms easily, especially at the point where the cable nipple is held. A lot of problems are prevented by taking the unit apart early in its life and applying a generous amount of the special grease specified by the manufacturer to everything that moves.

Adjust Sturmey-Archer 5-Speed Hub

On most versions of this hub, there is a bell crank mechanism on the LH side, while the RH side has the same nut with viewing port as found on the same manufacturer's 3-speed models. Verify whether the cable runs freely, the cable stops are firmly installed, and whether the bell crank and the control chain are exactly aligned with their respective cable sections. If the hub has not been lubricated in the last three months, do that first, after which it should be tried again. Once these points have

been corrected, no tools are required as a rule.

Procedure for models with two separate shifters:

1. Place the LH shifter in the position that releases tension on the LH cable, while turning the cranks at least half a revolution with the wheel lifted off the ground.

2. If necessary, adjust it so that it is just taut but not under tension.

3. Place the RH shifter in the intermediate position.

4. Shift the LH shifter until it fully tensions the cable.

5. Check all gears. If any do not work, adjust the RH adjuster a little looser or tighter.

Procedure for models with a single shifter:

1. Select the fourth gear.

Adjusting the Shimano 7-speed at the shifter. Note the use of a gear indicator, which is also finding its way into derailleur shifters. for the 94 season.

To replace the cable, or to remove the wheel, disconnect the cable from the control chain or rod that connects with the mechanism inside the hub.

2. Adjust the RH mechanism as described for the same manufacturer's 3-speed hub.

3. Place the shifter in the position for the fifth gear while turning the cranks half a revolution with the wheel raised off the ground.

4. The LH cable should now be tightened — adjust, if necessary.

5. Try out all the gears and re-adjust, if necessary.

Adjust Sachs 5-Speed Hub

This hub is always operated by means of a single shifter. No tools are needed for the adjustment, which has to be preceded by the usual check of the cables, shifter, guide and stops. If an old model has persistent shifter problems, replace the shifter.

Procedure:

1. Select the fifth gear while turning the cranks forward with the wheel raised off the ground.

2. Loosen the cable-adjusting clips on both sides, so the cables on

both sides of the hub are completely loose in this position.

3. Turn the cranks forward by at least one revolution with the wheel raised off the ground.

4. Put the cable adjusting clips on their pins so that the cables are just taut but not under tension.

5. Select the first gear, while turning the cranks forward with the wheel raised off the ground.

6. Check whether this gear engages properly.

7. If the first gear does not engage properly, return to the fourth gear and tighten the looser cables one notch, repeating steps 5–7 as necessary until the first gear works properly.

8. Check all the gears in turn, and re-adjust, if necessary.

Replace Shifter or Cable

This has to be done if the problem cannot be solved by means of adjustment and lubrication. If the cause is clearly not here either, the hub gear mechanism itself is at fault. If you are faced with this predicament, it will be easier to replace the entire wheel complete with hub. You can then take your time dismantling the old hub to see whether you can find an obviously defective part.

When replacing shifter or cable, it should be noted that each is basically designed for the same maker's hub. Just the same, there are adaptor pieces that allow the use of one manufacturer's cable with another manufacturer's adjusting mechanism. In the case of the 3-speed, it is often possible to use non-matching shifters. Five-speeds can be operated with two separate 3-speed shifters of any make instead of the original complicated 5-position shifter. By way of tools, you'll need a screwdriver and a crescent wrench.

Removal procedure:

1. Loosen the cable adjuster at the hub.

2. Pull the cable back towards the shifter for enough slack.

3. Pull the shift lever in as far as possible (or, in the case of a 5-speed, open it up to gain access) and remove the nipple out of the recess in the shifter. Then hold the cable and push the lever up into the high position.

4. Pull the cable back out of the shifter and off the guides and stops.

5. Remove the part that has to be replaced (cable or shifter).

Installation procedure:

1. When replacing the lever, install it in the right position.

2. Pull the shift lever in as far as possible or, in the case of a 5-speed lever, open it up to gain access. Feed the nipple in and hook it in the recess in the shifter.

Shimano 7-speed system: line up the color-coded marks on the control ring and the hub body in 4th gear.

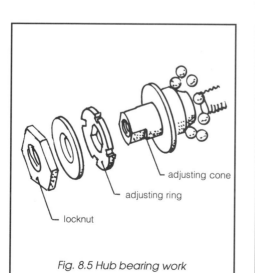

adjusting cone

adjusting ring

locknut

Fig. 8.5 Hub bearing work

Sachs 7-speed hub: the one control is placed inside the other at the hub, and they are combined at the click box.

3. Hold the cable pulled taut and place it over the various guides and stops.

4. At the hub, attach it to the control chain or the bell crank.

5. Adjust the gears as described above.

Adjust Hub Bearings

The gear hub's ball bearings must be maintained just like those of other hubs. Actually, the adjustment procedure is quite easy once you have the manufacturer's special wrench which is usually supplied with the bike or the hub. Basically it's a cup-and cone ball bearing like any other one, and any adjustments are done on the LH side.

Procedure:

1. Loosen the LH axle nut 2–3 turns to the left.

2. Loosen the locknut 1–2 turns.

3. First tighten the adjusting nut for the cone fully, then back it off to the left by a quarter turn.

4. Hold the adjusting nut in this position and tighten the locknut.

5. Tighten the axle nut, while keeping the wheel centrally positioned.

6. Check the bearing to make sure it is neither too loose nor too tight, and re-adjust if necessary.

Adjust 7-Speed Hubs

Gear hubs with 7 speeds and built-in back-pedaling brake are made by both Sachs and Shimano. The general maintenance instructions correspond closely to those for 5-speed models. The controls for the Sachs unit are contained in the *click box*, a plastic housing on the outside of the hub, and any adjusting is done there. This box can simply be unhooked if the wheel has to be removed. The Shimano model's mechanism is contained in a narrow disk between the chain and the RH drop-out, requiring the removal of the cables from the adjustment mechanism — and subsequent readjustment of the gears — if the wheel has to be removed.

Adjusting procedure:

1. Make sure the cable is not pinched or damaged.

2. Select the first gear and turn the cranks one turn.

3. On Sachs hubs, pull the clip box off the pin protruding from the axle, then push it back on until the cable is taut.

4. On Shimano models, turn in the adjuster until the cable is taut.

5. Shift into each of the other gears and return to the first gear, then fine-tune the adjustment.

Gearing Range Adaptation

Although the ratios between the individual gears can not be varied in the case of hub gearing, the entire range can easily be shifted up or down. This is done by replacing the cog by a smaller or larger one, with fewer or more teeth respectively. These days, most systems are supplied with a 46-tooth chainring in the front and a 22-tooth cog in the back. Assuming a tire outside diameter of 685 mm, this results in a middle, or direct-drive, gear of 56 in. (development 4.50 m).

The entire range of gears can be lowered for more uphill gears by replacing the cog by one with, e.g., 23 or 24 teeth. Alternately, it may be raised by using a rear cog with, e.g., 20 or 21 teeth. Such minor changes can easily be made without changing the length of the chain (merely move the wheel forward or backward a little and tighten it in its new position. If the chain will not reach or hangs too loose, refer to Chapter 6 for instructions on adding or removing links.

Overhaul Gear Hub

Although three-speed hubs, and even five-speeds, are not very expensive as sophisticated bicycle components go, overhauling may still be worthwhile when adjustment and lubrication does not solve the problem. The reason to do this lies mainly in the high cost (or the time-consuming work) involved in rebuilding the wheel, which will be necessary when replacing the hub. Yet it is beyond the scope of this book to describe this job in detail for each model separately.

In fact, it will be smarter to merely go about it systematically, referring to the various illustrations included on these pages.

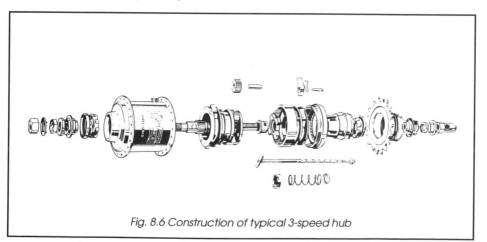

Fig. 8.6 Construction of typical 3-speed hub

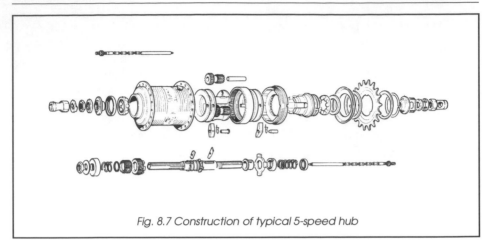

Fig. 8.7 Construction of typical 5-speed hub

Procedure:

1. Undo the control cable at the hub, and remove the wheel from the bike.

2. Remove the control rod or the bell crank.

3. Place the wheel down flat in front of you, the chain side up.

4. Remove the cog, as described in Chapter 6, *The Drivetrain.*

5. Remove the locknut and the lock washer.

6. Remove the bearing cone and the parts that become accessible.

And now you're on your own, because things get different for the various models. Just work systematically, and if necessary make notes as to the sequence in which things were installed, so you can later get it back together. If it's any consolation, this is the way I go about it myself, and I've always been able to get the hub back in working order eventually.

Replace any damaged parts and lubricate before reassembling. See the description in Chapter 6, *The Drivetrain* for instructions on installing the freewheel mechanism. Adjust the bearings carefully. Finally, when you have reinstalled the wheel, proceed as for adjusting, described previously for the make and model in question.

CHAPTER 9

Rim Brakes

Bicycle brakes come in two major types — rim brakes and hub brakes — but the former are by far the more common. Even among rim brakes, there are two distinct types, namely calliper and stirrup brakes, but again, the latter are very rare indeed these days. The vast majority of modern bikes come with some kind of cable-operated calliper brakes, while the rod-operated stirrup brakes are now quit rare. Hub brakes will be treated separately in Chapter 10.

On all rim brakes, two brake pads are pushed against the rim. Among caliper brakes, sidepull and centerpull brakes are used on road bikes and installed as complete units. Cantilever brakes and cam-operated models are used on mountain bikes, hybrids and some touring bikes. They consist of individual brake arms that are mounted on bosses brazed, welded or bonded on the front fork at the front and either the chain stays or the seat stays at the rear. The more recently introduced low-profile cantilever brakes do not protrude as far as conventional models.

At the rear, cantilever brakes are always installed on the seat stays, whereas other mountain bike brakes are sometimes mounted underneath the chain stays. For mountain bikes, there is also a centerpull type, called U-brake, with individual brake arms mounted on pivot bosses mounted on the frame or the front fork.

All of the common brakes are connected to the hand lever by

The two most commonly used brakes these days: sidepull (left) and cantilever (right).

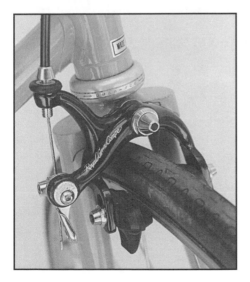

means of a flexible Bowden cable. Usually, the LH lever controls the front brake, while the RH lever operates the rear brake, although they can be reversed according to your preference.

On many mountain bikes, the cable for the front brake runs either over a roller mounted under the handlebar stem or through a hole in the stem. Both solutions are a bit of a pain, since they require a full brake readjustment whenever the handlebar position has been changed. It is better to install an anchor that is clamped between the lock washer and the locknut of the head-set.

Cantilever, centerpull and U-brakes have a connecting cable, also called straddle cable, between the two brake arms. This cable must be kept as short as possible (top angle of cable triangle as big as possible) if the two sides are to be pushed together enough for adequate brake force. Shimano's versions don't have a conventional straddle cable: instead, the main cable runs to one of the brake arms and the second brake arm is connected to it via a short cable and a connecting clamp.

Brake Maintenance

From a maintenance standpoint, the brakes should be considered as complete systems, each incorporating levers, control cables and various

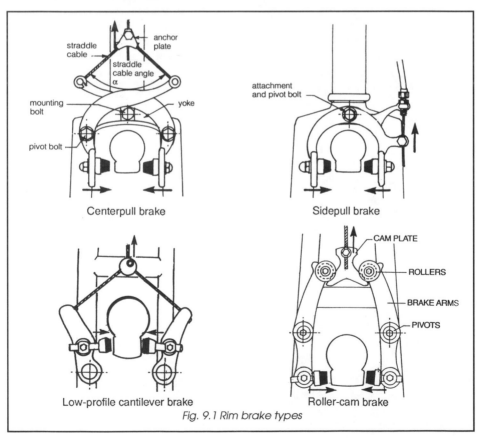

Centerpull brake

Sidepull brake

Low-profile cantilever brake

Roller-cam brake

Fig. 9.1 Rim brake types

pieces of mounting hardware, as well as the brake itself. In fact, brake problems are most often due to inadequacies of some component in the control system. Consequently, it will be necessary to approach the problem systematically, trying to isolate the fault by checking off one component after the other.

When the brakes work inconsistently, often with associated vibrations or squealing, the cause is usually found either in dirt and grease on the rims, loosely mounted fittings, or incorrect brake pad positioning. First check the condition of the rims, then the attachments of brake pads, brake arms, brake units, cables, anchors and levers. If the rim is dented, there is usually no other solution than to replace it, while all other causes can usually be eliminated quite easily.

Adjust Brake Pads

This simple job is often not only the solution to squealing, rumbling or vibrating noises, but may also solve inadequate braking performance and prevent serious mishaps. As the brake pad wears, its position relative to the rim changes. On a cantilever brake, it moves radially inward — farther away from the tire and toward the spokes — while it moves up towards the tires on all other brakes. If left unchecked, chances are it will eventually hit the spokes or the tire instead of the rim.

To prevent this, it is not enough to follow the systematic brake test described below regularly: you also have to check the position of the brake pads as they contact the rim, and readjust them if they don't align.

In addition, it is preferable if the front end of the brake pad is about 1–2 mm closer to the rim than the rear. This is to compensate for the deformation of the brake arm as brake force is applied, which tends to twist the back of the brake pad in. Only when you adjust them this way, referred to as *toed in*, will the brake force be equally distributed over the entire length of the brake pad.

Tools and equipment:
• pliers
• 5 mm Allen key
• 9 mm wrench

Procedure:

1. Loosen the nut or bolt that holds the brake pad to the brake arm by about one turn.

2. While applying the corresponding brake lever with modest hand force, move the brake pads in the position illustrated, then increase lever force. You may have to twist the brake pad and the underlying spherical and cupped washers —

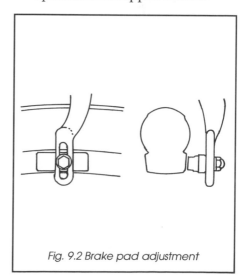

Fig. 9.2 Brake pad adjustment

or whatever other device is provided for angular adjustment — to achieve this position.

3. Place a small piece of cardboard, about 1 mm ($\frac{1}{32}$–$\frac{1}{16}$ in.) thick between the brake pad and the rim, over the back 12 mm ($\frac{1}{2}$ in.) of the brake pad.

4. Holding the brake pad against the side of the rim firmly with the pliers, making sure it does not shift from its correct position, tighten the bolt fully.

5. Check to make sure the brake works correctly, and fine-tune the adjustment if necessary.

Brake Test

In order to verify their condition and effectiveness, test the brakes according to the following systematic procedure at regular intervals — about once a month under normal condi-

This is how far the brake lever should clear the handlebars when full force is applied.

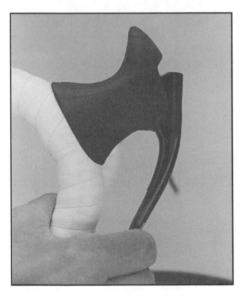

tions. The idea is to establish whether the deceleration achieved with each brake is as high as the physical constraints of the bicycle's geometry will allow. Tools are not needed for this test.

Procedure:

1. Ride the bike at a brisk walking speed (about 8 km/h, or 5 m.p.h.) on a straight, level surface without traffic.

2. Apply the rear brake hard. If the rear wheel skids, you have all the braking you can use in the rear — a deceleration of 3.5 m/sec^2.

3. Repeat the procedure with the front brake. But be careful – you don't want to go over the handlebars. If the rear wheel starts to lift off, a deceleration of 6.5 m/sec^2 has been reached, and that's as much as you'll ever want. Let go of the front brake again.

Brake System Inspection

If one brake or the other fails the test described above, check the entire brake system and adjust or correct as necessary. Usually, no tools are needed for this inspection, but you may have to use a variety of items to solve individual problems uncovered this way.

Procedure:

1. Check to make sure the rim and the brake pads are clean. The presence of wet or greasy dirt plays havoc with their operation. Wipe clean or degrease the rim and scrape the brake pad with steel wire wool.

2. Check whether the cables move freely and are not pinched or damaged. In the case of special controls, such as hydraulics or pull rods, check them for correct operation and installation. Clean, free and lubricate or replace cables that don't move freely. Repair or replace anything else found wanting.

3. Inspect the levers — they must be firmly installed and there must be at least 2 cm (¾ in.) clearance between lever and handlebars when the brake is applied fully. If necessary, tighten, lubricate, and adjust.

4. Make sure the brake arms themselves are free to move without resistance, and that they are returned to clear the wheel fully by the spring tension when the lever is released. If necessary, loosen, adjust, lubricate, overhaul or replace.

Right: Adjusting the brake pad position on the rim. It must completely lie on the rim when the brake lever is pulled. The attachment hardware varies between different models.

Adjust Brakes

Roughly the same operation is followed for all types of calliper brakes, although the adjustment mechanisms may be installed in different positions. By way of tools, it is handy to have a pair of needle-nose pliers to adjust a centerpull brake, while you may need an Allen key or a wrench to fit the cable clamping nut on all models.

The most common type of brake adjustment is that required to tighten the cable a little in order to compensate for brake pad wear. This operation is about the same, whatever type of brake you have. First carry out the brake pad adjustment mentioned above, though. If you don't, there is a risk of the brake pad sooner or later slipping off the side of the rim, hitting either the tire or the spokes.

Tools and equipment:
• 5 mm Allen key

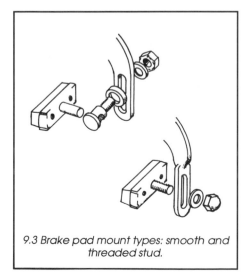

9.3 Brake pad mount types: smooth and threaded stud.

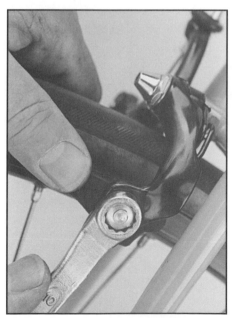

- 9 mm wrench
- pliers

Procedure:

1. If the brake does not perform adequately, the cable tension has to be increased. Do that initially by tightening the cable adjuster by two turns.

2. Verify whether the brake now engages fully when 2 cm (¾ in.) clearance remains between lever and handlebars.

3. If the correct adjustment cannot be achieved within the adjusting range of the cable adjuster, first screw it in all the way, then pull the cable further and tighten the clamping bolt again. On the centerpull brake this can be done by wrapping the cable around the needle nose pliers and twisting it further. Now fine-tune with the adjuster.

Adjusting a brake at its barrel adjuster.

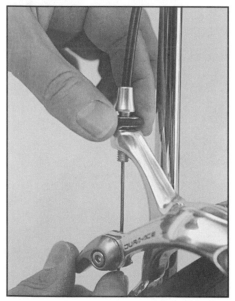

4. If after all this adjusting the brake finally transmits enough tension but does not clear the rim adequately when disengaged, you will have to check all parts of the system and replace or overhaul as necessary.

Procedure for roller-cam brake

This particular type of brake, although not used very much any more, has some peculiar features that make it extremely effective for touring bikes and mountain bikes—but only if adjusted correctly. And its adjustment is quite different from that of other brakes. Carry out this procedure whenever the brake does not seem to be operating properly. Before making any changes, make sure the rim is clean: sometimes it is merely a matter of a greasy and slippery rim.

Tools and equipment:
- 5 mm Allen key
- 9–10 mm wrench
- 14 mm cone wrench

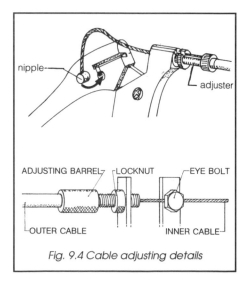

Fig. 9.4 Cable adjusting details

Procedure:

1. Check the alignment of the brake pads on the rim: they must lie flat and fully contact the side of the rim when the lever is pulled hard.

2. Check whether the brake pads protrude the right distance from the brake arm. Measure the distance between the brake arm mounting pivots and determine the correct protrusion from the following table:

Dimension A ...	Dimension B
92 mm	29 mm
90 mm	28 mm
88 mm	27 mm
86 mm	26 mm
84 mm	25 mm

If the dimensions do not match, adjust until they do.

3. Check the centering of the brake pads, after first making sure the rim itself is centered between the frame stays (or fork blades, if the brake is used in the front) and correcting if necessary. If the distance between the side of the rim and the brake pad is different on each side, adjust.

4. The centering of the brake is a function of the spring tension, and most models have two separate springs that can be adjusted individually. To do this, first check to make sure the fixing nuts on the brake arm pivot bolts are tight, then use a 14 mm cone wrench (or any flat open-ended wrench of this size) to turn the pivot bushings immediately under the brake arms by only a very slight angular amount, until the two brake arms are centered relative to the rim.

5. Sometimes it is necessary to readjust the brake pad location, following points 3–4 above, after this operation, so the brake pads are the same distance and touch the rim correctly.

Centering Brakes

One of the most frustrating problems can be the off-centered position of a brake, always rubbing along the rim

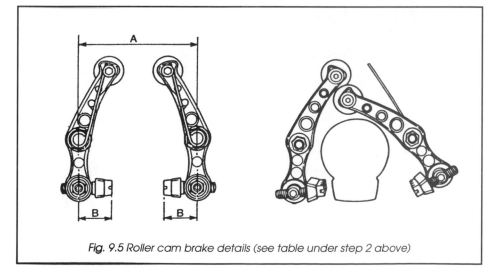

Fig. 9.5 Roller cam brake details (see table under step 2 above)

on one side while clearing it on the other. If the problem is intermittent, first try to alleviate it by truing the wheel (see Chapter 4). If the problem is constant, the solution will be different depending on the kind of brake you have.

Centerpull brake:

On this type of brake, it is generally a simple matter of twisting the yoke on which the brake arms are installed in the right orientation.

1. First make sure the brake is firmly attached, tightening the mounting bolt if necessary, while depressing the lever and holding the brake centered.

2. If the brake is properly fastened and still off-set, take a big screwdriver and a hammer. Place the screwdriver on the pivot point that is too high and lightly tap it with the hammer.

3. Repeat or correct until the brake is centered.

Sidepull brake:

Here the problem is due to the stubbornness of the mounting bolt, always twisting back into an off-center position. Straightening is easier said than done: it will find its way back to this wrong position the next time the brake is applied. Some brake models come with a special adjusting tool with which the mounting bolt is repositioned, each of them with its own instructions. There is also a universal tool, which may work on brakes without their own special tool: place each of the pins inside a loop of the spring and twist in the appropriate direction. On other models, for which no tool is provided, proceed as follows:

Centering brakes:
Left: centerpull brake;
Right cantilver brake.

Tools and equipment:
- 13–14 mm cone wrench
- 6 mm Allen key

Procedure:

1. If the mounting bolt has flats between the brake and the fork or the frame, place the cone wrench on these flats and the second wrench or Allen key on the nut at the end of the mounting bolt. If not, put a wrench on each end of the mounting bolt.

2. Older brakes may have two nuts on the top of the mounting bolt — the outside nut if you have to turn clockwise, the inside one to turn counterclockwise.

3. To twist the mounting bolt, turn both tools simultaneously.

If after all this the problem remains or returns, install a flat, thin steel washer between the brake body and the fork or rear stay bridge (or the shaped spacer installed there). This will provide a smooth 'un-biased' surface that can be twisted into the desired position, rather than getting stuck in existing incorrect indentations.

Cantilever brake:

1. Most models have a hexagonal recess in one of the pivots that is turned one way or the other, essentially tensioning a spring that is hidden inside the bushing.

2. Other models have 14 mm flats between the pivot boss and the brake arms, and they can be adjusted by turning the pivot bolt with a matching cone wrench.

3. On most Dia-Compe brakes, loosen the pivot bolt and turn the bushing behind it with a 13 mm cone wrench, and tighten the bolt again.

4. On older versions without a centering screw, bend one of the springs that spread the brake levers in or out a little, using needle-nose pliers.

U-brake:

This kind of brake usually has a small adjusting screw in one of the brake arms that can be turned in a little to bring that arm in, or loosened to bring the other one in. If not, dismantle the brake and bend the spring in or out until it is symmetrical.

Centering a modern sidepull brake using a cone wrench. Other models may require special tools and some are equipped with a grub screw to fix them in place.

Roller-cam brake:

This is the most popular form of what I referred to as a cam-operated brake. This brake usually comes with a similar little adjusting screw on one of the brake arms that is tightened or loosened to center the brake arms.

Overhaul or Replace Brake

Especially if the bike is frequently used in bad weather or off-road, this work is recommended once a year — or whenever the brake gives unsatisfactory performance and adjustment does not solve the problem.

Although there are slight differences in the procedure as it applies to different brakes, you will find a general description here, including comments for specific models. Most comments apply to all brakes, though. This work is most easily car-

Most cantilever brakes have several different locations for the end of the spring. Choose the one that centers the brake best.

ried out while the wheel is removed. For easy wheel removal on brakes without quick-release, push the brake pads together just enough to unhook the cable (centerpull, U-brake or cantilever). On the roller-cam, remove the cam plate, then loosen the tip of one spring and spread the brake arms asymmetrically.

Tools and equipment:
- 13–14 mm cone wrench
- 5 mm Allen key
- needle-nose pliers

Removal procedure:

1. Pull the brake arms together at the brake pads and release the cable — on the roller-cam brake by twisting the cam plate out from between the rollers.

2. Check condition of the cable and replace if necessary: remove the cable anchor clamp using a wrench on the nut and an Allen key on the bolt part. Pull the cable out, and later insert the new one. If an end cap is installed on the end of the cable, it must be pulled off with needle-nose pliers — I recommend soldering or crimping the end of the cable to prevent fraying, following the instructions under *Replace Brake Cable.*

3. Unscrew the fixing nut on top of the brake arm pivot bolt of each brake arm. In the case of a sidepull or centerpull brake, remove the whole unit.

4. Using the needle-nose pliers, remove the upper end of the spring of each brake arm from its seating, then pull the brake arm,

the spring and the bushing off the pivot stud.

5. Clean, inspect and if necessary repair or replace any damaged parts. In particular, remove any rust from the pivot stud of the pivot boss, then apply some vaseline or bearing grease to this location. On the roller-cam, you may remove the rollers from the brake arms, and install these again after inspection, cleaning and lubrication.

6. If appropriate, remove the brake pads and their fixing bolts, in order to clean and if necessary replace them (if the brake pads are badly worn).

Installation procedure:

1. After ascertaining that all parts are functional, clean and, where appropriate, lightly greased, first put the springs on the pivot studs, with the long arms of the spring pointing up and to the inside.

2. Install the adjusting bushing over the top of the spring around the stud of each mounting boss, the cylindrical bushing part protruding.

3. Install the brake arms on the adjusting bushings, followed by the washer and the nut or the bolt.

4. In the case of a roller-cam brake, hook the end of the spring into its seating at the end of the roller pin of each brake arm.

5. Push the brake pads together and reinstall the cam plate between the rollers (on the roller-cam) or the

connecting cable (on other models).

6. If appropriate, readjust the cable tension by adjusting at the brake lever or — if the deviation is significant — by clamping the anchor plate (U-brake or cantilever brake) or the cam plate (on the roller-cam brake) at a different point on the cable.

7. In the case of sidepull or center-pull brakes, re-install the complete unit.

8. Adjust the brakes.

Brake Controls

Almost without exception, rim brakes are operated via handlebar-mounted levers via flexible cables. Exceptions are hydraulically operated brakes (with oil-filled tubes instead of cables) and stirrup brakes (which use rigid rods instead of cables). The following sections deal

This is how you reach the hidden mounting bolt of a road bike brake lever.

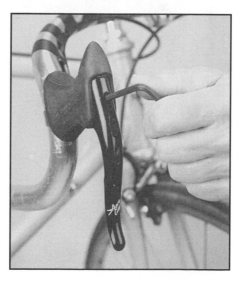

with the maintenance of levers and cables.

Adjust Brake Lever

Although there are a number of different makes and models within the categories of road and mountain bike brake levers, the similarities are generally so great that the following general description covers all but the most unusual models. All are designed to fit standard 22.2 mm (7/8 in.) diameter handlebars as used on all regular mountain bikes. Any bike with a different diameter handlebar also requires a modified or custom-built clamp for the brake lever.

Levers for simple bikes with flat handlebars have an external mounting clamp (referred to as hook strap), while mountain bikes have a one-piece clamp that is accessible from the outside. Drop handlebars call for an internal clamp (referred to as pull

On Shimano STI systems, and similar systems from Sachs and Campagnolo, the brake levers are combined with the shifters.

strap) accessible after depressing the lever. The cable on most modern levers for drop handlebars no longer comes out the top but at the bottom near the clamp and is routed along the handlebars.

The brake lever must be installed so that it can be easily reached and pulled in so far that the brake is fully applied when a gap of about 20 mm (3/4 in.) remains between the brake lever and the handlebars at the tightest point. There are four forms of adjustment that apply to the brake lever:
☐ mounting position
☐ reach
☐ cable routing
☐ cable tension

Tools and equipment:
• 5 mm Allen key
• 9–10 mm wrench
• small screwdriver (for older models)

Procedure — position adjustment:

1. Determine in which direction the brake lever should be moved or rotated to provide adequate and comfortable operation.

2. Establish whether any other parts installed on the handlebars (e.g. shift levers) may have to be moved in order to allow moving the brake lever to the desired position. Loosen these parts, so they can be easily moved.

3. Using the Allen key or wrench, loosen the the clamp that holds the lever to the handlebars by one or two turns, then twist or slide the lever to its desired location and tighten the clamping bolt

again. Whatever you do, make sure the lever does not extend beyond the end of the handlebars. You want to avoid accidental brake application while passing closely by any objects in your path behind which the brake levers might get caught.

4. Most road bikes have an internal bolt that can be reached once the lever is pulled, preferably after removing the cable. On old models it requires a screwdriver, while more recent versions require the use of a 5 mm Allen key. Make sure not to unscrew this bolt all the way, because it will be hard to reinstall.

5. Retighten any other components that may have been moved to new locations; make sure all parts are really in their most convenient position and are properly tightened.

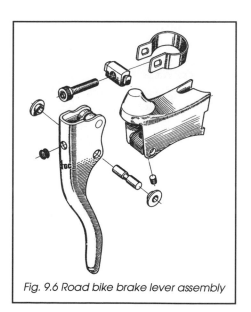

Fig. 9.6 Road bike brake lever assembly

Procedure — reach adjustment:

1. Most (though not all) mountain bike brake levers are equipped with a set-screw that can be turned in or out in order to limit the range of travel of the brake lever as appropriate to the reach of your hand.

2. Check the distance between the handlebars and the brake lever in unapplied position compared with the maximum comfortable reach of your hand. In general, it should be opened as far as possible commensurate with the size of your hand, since a larger reach allows the most effective brake application and the most accurate adjustment of the brake cable.

3. If adjustment is necessary, tighten the range adjusting screw to reduce the range (i.e. the maximum opening position), or loosen it to increase the range.

4. Check to make sure the brake can be applied properly, and adjust the brake cable, following the appropriate instructions below, if necessary.

Replace or Overhaul Brake Lever

Brake levers should be matched both to the brake mechanism and to the handlebars used: even for the same brake, different levers are designed for drop handlebars and for straight or upright bars. Children's bikes should be equipped with levers designed for that specific purpose, since the child's hand is not generally big enough to reach an adult lever.

Before removing or installing a brake lever, the handlebar tape or the handgrips must be removed from the handlebars. It will be necessary to loosen the brake cable (as described above) if the lever is to be replaced by another one. Refer to the exploded views for overhauling. Usually a stiff operating lever can be freed by replacing the bushings or by bending the metal around the pivot out a little. If not, you may have to replace the entire lever.

Tools and equipment:
• screwdriver or Allen key (depending on type of internal attachment bolt, reached when the lever is pulled).

Removal procedure:

1. Release tension on the brake cable (either with the quick- release, with the adjustment mechanism, or the cable attachment bolt).

2. Pull the lever; push the cable inside the lever to the side to gain access to the internal bolt. Loosen

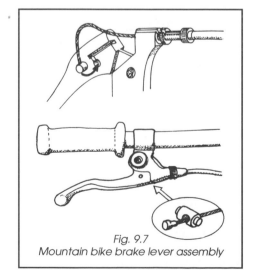

Fig. 9.7
Mountain bike brake lever assembly

the bolt about three full turns — just not so far that it comes out of its special nut, since it would be hard to get back in before installing the lever. The strap with which the lever is clamped around the handlebars opens up a little this way.

3. Push the lever assembly off the handlebar ends, in a twisting movement if it becomes tight, loosening the bolt further if it will not come off any other way.

Installation procedure:

1. Make sure the lever used is correct for the handlebars and the brake installed on the bike. Replace the cable if it is not in perfect condition.

2. Unscrew the internal bolt in the lever just far enough to loosen the attachment strap — not so far that it will come out of the special nut: if it does, it will be tricky to put it back in.

3. Slide the lever over the end of the handlebars into the right position. Check the position to make sure it can be reached and fully contracted easily with the whole hand — moving it further up or down the bend in the handlebars or angling it in or out will often improve these things. If the strap will not fit around the bars, it is the wrong size.

4. Tighten the bolt when the bars are in the right position; then install the cable as described above, making any adjustments to the brake that may be called for.

Note:

Some cheap brake levers are attached with an external clamp. These are potential hazards, and I recommend replacing them by a model with a strap attachment as described here. If you must install the type with external clamp, it will be obvious how that's done.

Extension Levers

Although less so than a few years ago many cheaper ten-speed bikes still come equipped with extension levers, with which the brakes can be operated from the top of the drop handlebar. The soundest advice is probably to remove them, yet many riders feel safer with them, and my zeal for their reform is less firm than my desire to a least teach them how these things should be used to their best advantage.

There are different types, but almost all work similar, pivoted

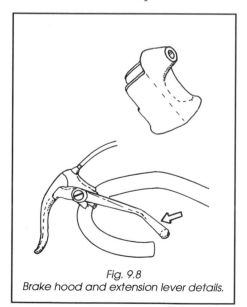

Fig. 9.8
Brake hood and extension lever details.

around the main brake lever pivot point, and the other lever either inserted between the brake lever mount and the lever proper, or attached directly to another pivot on the lever.

Adjust the brake lever assembly in such a way that both the regular lever and the extension lever can be reached comfortably and will not bottom out before the brake is applied fully as described in the checking procedure under *Rim Brake Adjustments*. This usually requires slightly different position and angle on the bend of the handlebars, and that may require shifting or replacing the handlebar tape.

Extension levers are not usually very rigid (which is also their inherent drawback), so it will be possible to bend them into a more favorable shape. When you are in an emergency, and have to brake very hard and suddenly, you should use the regular brake lever, so that full braking force is applied. If you remove the extension, also replace the overlong pivot bolt by a regular model to avoid injury.

Brake Hoods

Brake levers for drop handlebars without extension levers generally come equipped with soft rubber hoods. These provide significant comfort when riding in such a position that the hands are just on top of the brake lever mounts. Install, replace or remove the hood when the cable is disconnected. When you remove the extension levers, I suggest you add such as rubber hood at the time — almost any make of hood will fit any make of lever, provided a regular

brake lever pivot bolt is installed.
When installing handlebar tape, lift
up the hood to allow you to wrap
closely around the brake lever mount.

Adjust Brake Cable

The main brake adjustment—the
only one usually required from time
to time to compensate for brake pad
wear—is that of the brake cable. To
adjust the brake cable tension, either
the lever or the brake unit is
equipped with a barrel adjuster. In
case the adjusting range of this
device is not adequate, the attachment of the cable to the brake itself
can be changed. The latter adjustment depends on the type of brake
used, but the instructions can be
generalized enough to cover most
situations.

*When installing or adjusting the cable of a
centerpull brake, you can tension the
cable by wrapping it around needle-
nosed pliers.*

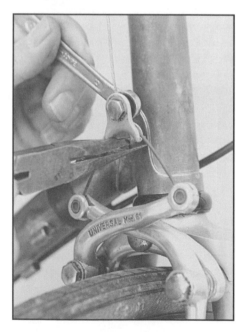

Tools and equipment:
• needle-nose pliers
• 5 mm Allen key or 9 mm wrench

Procedure:

1. If the brake does not apply adequate force when the lever is
   pulled, the cable must be
   tightened. If, on the other hand,
   the brake seems to be applied too
   soon — if the brake scrapes the
   side of the rim when the lever is
   not pulled — it should be slack-
   ened a little.

2. To tighten the brake cable, hold
   the locknut and screw the barrel
   adjuster out by several turns. Then
   hold the barrel adjuster in place,
   while screwing in the locknut.

3. To release the brake cable, hold
   the barrel adjuster and back off the
   locknut by several turns, then
   screw the barrel adjuster in further, and finally tighten the locknut, while holding the barrel
   adjuster to stop it from turning.

4. Check and readjust, if necessary,
   until operation of the brake is optimal.

5. If the adjusting range of the barrel
   adjuster is not adequate, screw it
   in all the way, after having backed
   off the locknut fully. Then proceed
   to adjust the clamping position of
   the cable at the brake.

6. The end of the cable at the brake
   unit itself is clamped onto an
   anchor by means of either an eye
   bolt or a pinch plate held under a
   bolt-and-nut combination. Loosen
   the nut of this unit and pull the
   cable through a little further, then
   clamp it in properly at the new

position by tightening the nut while holding the bolt.

7. Check once more and adjust the barrel adjuster at the brake lever if necessary.

Straddle cable note:

Sometimes cantilever brakes don't work properly because the angle between the two halves of the straddle cable is too sharp. Keeping the straddle cable clamped in as short as possible while still clearing the tire will improve its performance. If on the brake in question one end of the main cable runs through to one brake arm and the straddle cable is replaced by a single short cable connecting the second brake arm to a clamped-on anchor plate, loosen it and clamp it closer in, making sure the two cable ends run symmetrically.

Replace Brake Cable

This should be done about once a year — or whenever it is pinched, corroded or otherwise damaged, especially if signs of broken strands are in evidence. Make sure you get a model that has the same kind of nipple (visible inside the lever) as the old one.

Tools and equipment:
• 5 mm Allen key or 9 mm wrench
• cable cutters
• grease
• soldering equipment or crimping tool

Removal procedure:

1. Release tension on the brake by squeezing the brake arms against the rim, then unhook the connecting cable (U-brake or cantilever brake) or the cam plate (roller-cam brake).

2. Unscrew the eye bolt or clamp nut that holds the cable to the connecting plate, the cam plate or the brake itself (depending on the type of brake), making sure not to lose the various parts.

3. Push the cable through towards the lever, then pull it out once enough slack is generated, catching any pieces of outer cable and end pieces.

4. Screw the adjuster and the locknut at the lever in and leave them in such a position that their slots are aligned with the slot in the lever housing, so the cable can be lifted out.

5. Remove the cable, dislodging the nipple from the lever.

Cable attachment detail and cutting the cable on a modern sidepull brake.

Installation procedure:

1. Establish whether the outer cable is still intact and replace it if necessary, cutting it to length in such a way that no hook is formed at the end (bending the metal of the spiral back if necessary).

2. Lubricate the inner cable with grease.

3. Place the nipple in the lever and guide the cable through the slot in the lever, the various guides and stops, and the sections of casing.

4. Attach the end in the eye bolt or clamp nut at the brake.

5. Adjust the cable tension as described above.

6. If you have the equipment to do it, solder the strands of the inner cable together at the end to prevent fraying, before you cut it off.

7. Cut off the excess cable length, leaving about 2.5–3 cm (1–1¼ in.) projecting. This is best done with a special cable cutters, although it can be done with other sharp and strong pliers, such as diagonal cutters.

8. If you have not soldered the end of the cable, put a crimp on the end.

Stirrup and Other Rod-Operated Brakes

Stirrup brakes are still used on some traditional English bikes, as well as in much of the Third World. They are not operated by cables but by means of pull rods that connect the lever via a series of frame-mounted pivots to the brake arms, which are pulled radially in towards the inside of the rim. In some other parts of the world, you may find drum brakes operated the same way.

Left: Adjusting or installing the mounting and pivot bolt of a modern sidepull brake.

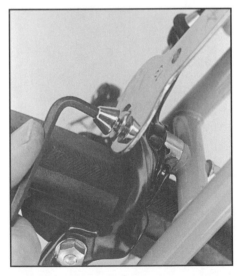

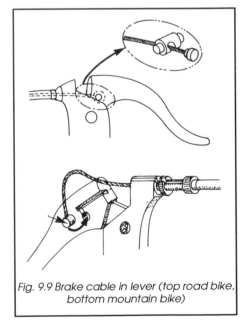

Fig. 9.9 Brake cable in lever (top road bike, bottom mountain bike)

Stirrup brakes and other rod-operated brakes are usually adjusted by means of a knurled round nut or a screw at the end of the rod where it is attached to the stirrup or the drum brake's activating lever. Apart from the usual brake pad maintenance, they should be lubricated at the pivot points once a month, at the same time each of the attachment nuts should be tightened. Straighten any bent rods and your rod-operated brakes will work forever.

Replace or Overhaul Brake

If the brake itself does not give good performance, especially if it does not operate gradually or will not open up fully after having been applied, it should be overhauled or replaced. Before you do, check whether the problem may be alleviated by adjusting, cleaning, lubricating or replacing the control cable and the lever, since these are the more frequent causes of braking problems.

Removal and installation of a typical modern sidepull brake.

Tools and equipment:
• wrench to fit attachment bolt
• wrench to fit nut on cable clamp bolt
• needle nose pliers
• to overhaul: small screwdriver and any wrenches to fit pivot bolts
• lubricant

Removal procedure:

1. Release tension on the brake cable (using quick-release, adjusting mechanism or cable clamp bolt). On centerpull and cantilever brakes, unhook the anchor plate from the straddle cable, and remove that cable.

2. Holding the brake mechanism in one hand, undo the mounting nut on the opposite side of the fork crown (front brake) or seat stay bridge (rear brake).

3. Remove the various spacers either side of the fork crown or seat stay bridge, while pulling the brake out of the hole. It may be necessary to release the cable altogether.

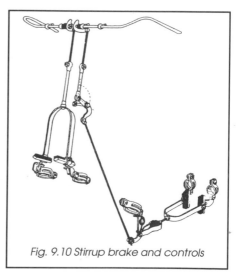

Fig. 9.10 Stirrup brake and controls

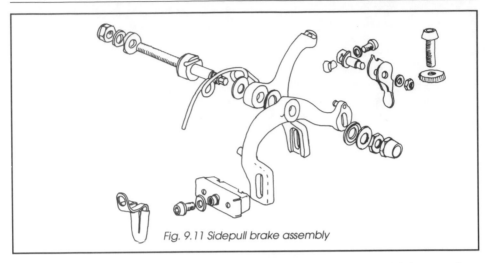

Fig. 9.11 Sidepull brake assembly

Overhauling procedure:

It is not possible to give step-by-step instructions for this work. Let the exploded views of the three most common brake types be your guide. Unhook and reinstall the return springs, using the small screwdriver. Replace any bent or damaged parts (your bike shop may keep a bin of discarded parts from which you can often get the appropriate replacement). Replace the nylon or PTFE (teflon) bushings at the pivots if they should

be damaged. Clean and lubricate the various parts before reassembling. Check for smooth operation and return movement before reinstalling.

Installation procedure:

1. Figure out where the various shaped spacers and washers should go. If you are installing a new brake, make sure the reach of the brake corresponds to the distance between the brake mounting hole and the position of the rim when the wheel is installed, and

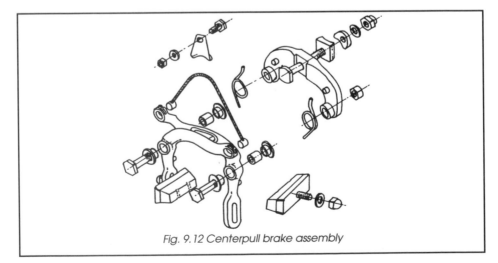

Fig. 9.12 Centerpull brake assembly

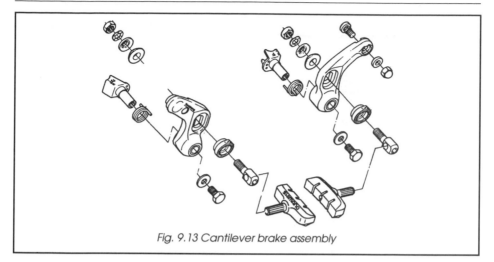

Fig. 9.13 Cantilever brake assembly

the brake is dimensioned to open up far enough to clear the width of the tire.

2. Put the washers or spacers that belong directly against the back of the brake in place on the mounting bolt; insert the bolt through the hole in the fork or the seat stay bridge; install the remaining spacers and washers; finally, install the nut.

3. Attach the cable, then adjust both cable and brake pad position as described in the appropriate instructions above. Make sure the brake is installed straight, so both brake pads are withdrawn equally far from the rim when the brake is released: loosen the mounting bolt slightly, straighten out, pull the lever firmly, hold the brake in that position, and tighten the bolt. Make final adjustments if necessary and don't forget to put the quick-release in the tightened position.

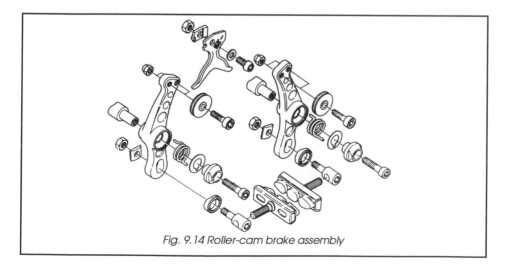

Fig. 9.14 Roller-cam brake assembly

Brake Squeal and Jitter

These two disturbing phenomena of
rim brake operation are at opposite
ends of the danger scale: squeal is
quite harmless, and really little more
than an embarrassment; brake jitter
can disturb steering and balancing
enough to cause a grave danger to
the rider.

A squealing brake may be
silenced by cleaning the rim, by
choosing a different brake pad
material, by using aluminum rims,
rather than steel versions, or by
toeing in the brake pads somewhat.
The latter operation brings the front
end of the brake pads a little closer to
the rim than the back — the braking
force will then straighten out the pad
again once the brake is applied. If the
brake is not adjustable in this direction (some cantilever brakes have
spherical inserts to do just that), you
will have to bend the brake arm into
the desired shape using two crescent
wrenches — if you have the nerve for
it.

Brake jitter is either caused by
looseness in the brake mounting bolt
or the pivots, by unevenness in the
side of the rim, or by excessive
flexibility in the fork, and may be aggravated by loose head-set bearings.
So those are the things to check and
to correct, although at least one of
these factors — flexibility in the fork
— cannot be eliminated, except by
replacing the entire fork. In my experience, fork flexibility should only
be seen as an aggravating factor, increasing the effect of other ones:
when the other problem is corrected,

the brake will not jitter, even with a
flexible fork. It is likely that choosing
different brake pad materials may
also alleviate the problem to some extent — experiment around, once you
have eliminated the most dangerous
causes and the symptoms have not
complete disappeared.

Tandem Brakes

Most tandems are (and indeed should
be) equipped with three brakes. As a
rule, two rim brakes — usually of the
cantilever design — are used in combination with a drum brake on the rear
wheel hub. All these brakes are
operated from the front handlebars,
leaving you more handles than hands,
if normal levers are chosen. There are
levers on the market which allow at-
taching two cables side-by-side. It is
usually recommended to control the
front rim brake separately with one
lever, the two rear brakes together with
the other.

Conversely, you may consider
the rear hub brake separately altogether, controlling it from a
separate lever, such as a guidonnet
lever mounted in the middle of the
handlebars or a "panic lever"
operated by the rider in the rear
(referred to as the stoker, while the
one in the front is called the captain
in bicycle jargon). It is even possible
to operate the rear drum brake from
a handlebar-end mounted gear shift
lever, as long as its pivot bolt is adjusted so tightly that it will indeed
hold adequately to retard the bike on
a long descent. Of course, you'll still
use the rim brakes in an emergency.

CHAPTER 10

Hub Brakes

They may not be used much these days, but you'll occasionally run into a bike with hub brakes. The coaster brake, usually referred to as back-pedaling brake in the U.K., is sometimes found on children's bikes. Drum and disk brakes are found on tandems as an auxiliary brake and some of the other brakes that will be handled in these pages are sometimes found on bikes intended for urban use.

Coaster Brake Maintenance

The major maintenance described here will be adjustment of the wheel bearings and other bearing work. These brakes tend to run hot when used vigorously over longer distances. In extreme cases, the lubricant burns out of the bearings. If this happens, you'll have to partly dismantle the bearings — after the hub has cooled — and repack them with the manufacturer's recommended special high-temperature grease.

Bearing adjustment procedure:

From time to time, check the bearings as described for the regular hub. If they are too loose or tight, adjust them without removing the wheel from the bike. The special wrench needed is usually supplied with the bike or the brake hub — if not, you can order it through a bike shop.

1. Loosen the LH axle nut 2–3 turns.

2. Loosen the round locknut with recesses about one turn.

Below: Connecting the lever that takes up the counter force on all hub brakes, here on a coaster brake. Right: Front wheel disk brake, necessary for mountain bikes with inverted type suspension forks..

3. If the hub is equipped with a square end on the RH axle end, turn it clockwise to loosen the axle, counterclockwise to tighten it.

4. On models without a square axle end, remove the locknut altogether and loosen the underlying shaped plate that engages the cone: to the left to loosen, to the right to tighten the bearing.

5. Tighten first the locknut, restraining the axle or the shaped plate; then tighten the axle nut.

Drum Brake Maintenance

These brakes are sometimes used on tandems and in some countries on touring and utility bikes. Maintenance operations include adjustment of the cable (or the control rod on models so operated) and the bearing. Very rarely, you may have to exchange the brake segments, or shoes, when the liners are worn or con-

All drum brakes are attached to the bike frame with a lever to counter the reaction forces.

taminated. In the latter case, dismantle the brake and remove the old shoes which can be relined or exchanged by a brake specialist.

Brake adjustment procedure:

Essentially, this is done as on any other hand-operated brake. The cable adjuster is used to increase the cable tension if the brake does not engage properly, and is loosened if it does not clear when the lever is released. As with the rim brake, the cable, the lever, the guides and the anchors must be checked, and if necessary cleaned, freed, lubricated or replaced when adjustment does not have the desired effect.

Bearing adjustment procedure:

The need for this is established as described in Chapter 4 for the regular hub. All you need is a 15 or 16 mm wrench and the special wrench that may be available for the particular model. The wheel may be left on the bike.

1. Loosen the axle nut on the control side by 3–4 turns.

2. Loosen the locknut by 1–2 turns, and lift the lock washer.

3. The adjusting plate, which engages the bearing cone, can now be turned to the right to tighten the bearings, or to the left to loosen them. Do not overtighten.

4. Hold the adjusting plate while tightening the locknut.

5. Tighten the axle nut, making sure the wheel is properly centered.

6. Check and repeat the adjustment if necessary.

Overhaul Drum Brake

This can become necessary when the bearings or the brake shoes are so far worn or damaged that adjusting does not solve the problem. The wheel must be removed from the bike, also disengaging the control cable and removing the bolt that holds the brake plate, or torque arm, to the fork or the chain stay.

Dismantling procedure:

1. Loosen the locknut completely and remove the lock washer.

2. Loosen the cone by means of the adjusting plate (or, after removing the latter, by means of a wrench), and remove it.

3. Remove the brake plate on which the entire mechanism is installed, while catching the bearing balls, which are usually contained in a retainer.

Maintenance and assembly procedure:

1. Clean and inspect all components:
   □ Replace the brake shoes if they are worn down to less than 3 mm (⅛ in.) at any point or when they are contaminated with oil and simply roughing them with steel wire wool does not restore them.
   □ Replace the ball bearings with their retainer and any other bearing components that are damaged (pitted, grooved, corroded).

2. Fill the bearing cups with bearing grease and push the bearing balls into the cups.

3. Apply just a little grease to the pivot and the cam on which the brake shoes sit.

4. Wipe excess grease away to make sure it cannot reach the brake liners or brake drum.

5. Install the brake plate with the brake shoes mounted on it.

6. Screw the cone in and tighten it with the aid of the adjusting plate.

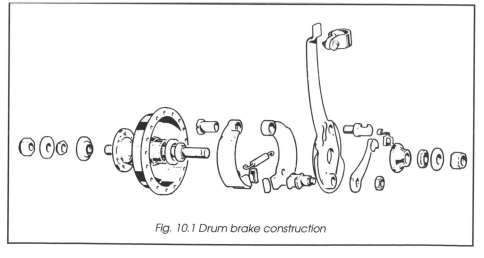

Fig. 10.1 Drum brake construction

7. Install the lock washer and the locknut, while holding the adjusting plate so it does not turn.

8. Check the bearing and adjust as necessary.

9. After installation of the wheel, check operation of the brake and adjust the cable tension, if necessary.

Hub Brake Controls

Except for the coaster brake, which is operated via the drivetrain by turning the cranks back, all other hub brakes are operated by means of hand levers similar to those described in Chapter 9 for rim brakes. On virtually all models sold in the U.S., the hand lever is connected to the brake via a Bowden cable, again as described in Chapter

Drum brake disassembled, showing the brake segments.

9. Some drum brakes are operated by means of pull rods that connect the lever via a series of frame-mounted pivots to the brake control lever.

Rod-operated brakes are usually adjusted by means of a knurled round nut or a screw at the end of the rod where it is attached to the stirrup or the drum brake's activating lever. Apart from the usual brake shoe maintenance, they should be lubricated at the pivot points once a month, at the same time each of the attachment nuts should be tightened. When properly treated, rod-operated systems are perhaps the most reliable available. Refer to the appropriate sections of Chapter 9 for all maintenance work on the brake controls.

Other Hub Brakes

All other types of hub brakes will be covered only for interest's sake. Due to their variety, no detailed maintenance instructions can be given here. Even so, with a little imagination and experience, gained on other bike maintenance operations, it will

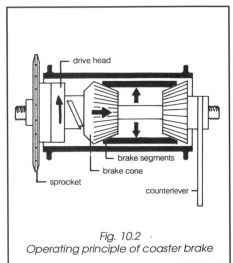

Fig. 10.2
Operating principle of coaster brake

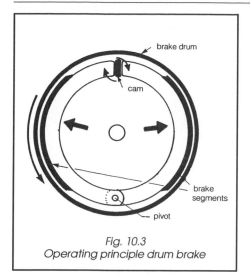

Fig. 10.3
Operating principle drum brake

place, since they vary quite a bit as regards construction details.

Most important is to check the cable tension adjustment as for regular rim brakes, and to make sure the disk does not get bent or otherwise damaged. Occasionally, clean the disk itself with a clean rag soaked in solvent, taking great care not to get any solvent or grease on the brake pads. As with all other hub brakes, the lever that connects the fixed part of the brake to the frame must be kept well tightened and securely reinstalled after any wheel removal or adjustment.

generally be possible to figure out what to do and how to go about it.

Disk brakes:

Disk brakes are even rarer than drum brakes, although they too are found on some tandems, and then also mainly on the rear wheel. I suggest requesting maintenance instructions from the manufacturer, if these were not supplied with the bike in the first

Separate drum brake:

This is a variant of the drum brake that is not an integral part of the hub but is screwed on the threaded end of a special hub by the same maker — usually Araya. It is intended only for use on the rear wheel, and its most common application is on tandems. Everything said about the conventional drum brake applies here too.

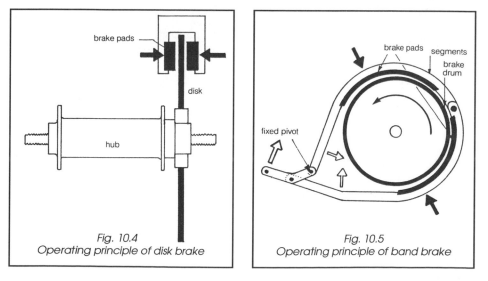

Fig. 10.4
Operating principle of disk brake

Fig. 10.5
Operating principle of band brake

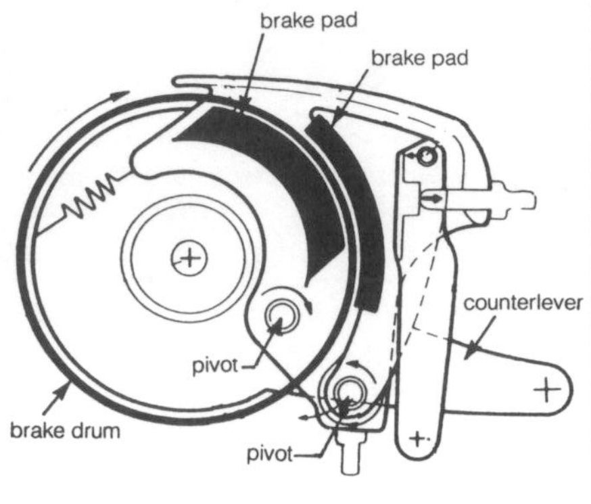

Fig. 10.6 Operating principle of
contraction-expansion brake

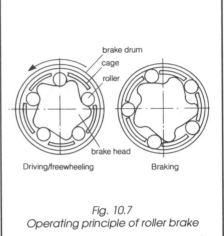

Fig. 10.7
Operating principle of roller brake

Band brake:

Seen mainly in the Far East, this is essentially a drum brake turned inside-out. A strap is pulled inward against the exterior of a brake drum, causing friction. Although it is a remarkably powerful brake, it suffers from overheating on longer descents because the surface that heats up is not directly exposed to the cooling air. This feature makes it inferior to the contracting drum brakes and most other rim and hub brakes.

Contraction-expansion brake:

This rare bird is sold by Bridgestone under the designation Dynex, but is rarely seen in the U.S. except on some old bikes. It combines the principles of the drum brake and the band brake, simultaneously pushing and pulling brake shoes against both the inside and the out-side of a heavy brake drum directly connected to a mounting plate with cooling fins. It works very well, due largely to the fact that the effect of fading in the one mode is compensated by increased braking force in the other.

Roller brake:

A little rear brake that is found primarily on cheap folding bikes and Formula-1 kid's bikes. Its operating principle is shown in Fig. 10.7 and corresponds to that of the unique freewheel first used in Fichtel & Sachs' coaster brakes. When pedaling back, the rollers travel up the inclined recesses and contact the brake mantle. It works very well for short-time braking but is unsafe for longer descents due to overheating on account of the brake's minuscule cooling surface.

CHAPTER 11

The Steering System

The parts of the steering system are the front fork, headset bearings, stem and handlebars. (The latter two parts are sometimes combined into a single welded unit.) We'll cover each of the components, starting at the most frequently necessary jobs.

Handlebars and Stem

The handlebars are generally clamped in the stem's clamping collar and the stem is held in the fork's steerer tube by means of a wedge-shaped or a cone-shaped device. This is pulled into the bottom of the stem with thexpander bolt, accessible from the top of the stem and usually equipped with a 6 mm hexagon recess for an Allen key. The collar of the stem is generally also provided with one or more Allen bolts to

clamp it around the handlebars, and often a grub screw (i.e. one without a head) to spread the collar apart.

The jobs you may have to do are adjusting the height, straightening the bars, and replacing either part. Most handlebars have a diameter of ⅞ in. (22.2 mm) at the ends and either 1 in. (25.4 mm), 1⅛ in. (26.6 mm), 26 mm, or 27 mm at the point where they are clamped into the

Front end with steering system of a modern mountain bike.

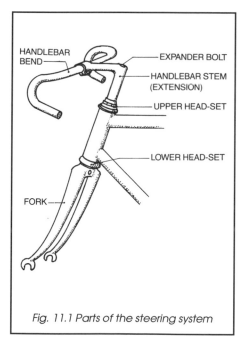

Fig. 11.1 Parts of the steering system

HANDLEBAR BEND
EXPANDER BOLT
HANDLEBAR STEM (EXTENSION)
UPPER HEAD-SET
LOWER HEAD-SET
FORK

stem. Make sure stem and handle-bars match when replacing either one.

Adjust Handlebars

This is required when the bike is set up for a different rider, when the position proves uncomfortable, or when the handlebars are not firmly in place.

Tools and equipment:
• 6 mm Allen key (or 12 mm wrench for older bikes with a hexagon-head expander bolt)
• sometimes a mallet or a hammer and a block of wood for protection

Procedure:

1. If the front brake cable is anchored at the stem, first loosen the brake to relax the cable tension.

2. To adjust the handlebar position, loosen the stem by unscrewing the expander bolt 2–3 turns.

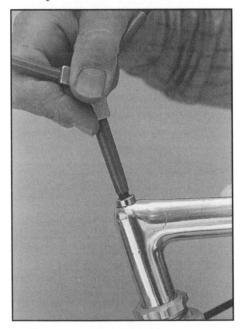

3. Straddle the front wheel, keeping it straight relative to the bike's frame, and put the handlebars in the required position as regards height and alignment, holding them steady with one hand.

4. If the stem won't turn or move, un-screw the expander bolt two more turns, lift the wheel off the ground, supporting the bike from the handlebars, then tap on the ex-pander bolt with the mallet, after which it will usually come loose. If it doesn't, enter some spray lubricant between the stem and the collar or locknut at the top of the headset and try again.

5. Put the handlebars in the desired position, but be careful if you are adjusting the height that the maxi-mum height marker engraved in the stem is not visible above the headset locknut, so it is clamped in securely.

6. Still holding firmly, tighten the ex-pander bolt.

Left: Undo the expander bolt to adjust or remove the handlebar stem.

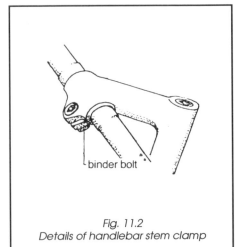

binder bolt

Fig. 11.2
Details of handlebar stem clamp

7. Verify whether the handlebars are now in the right position and make any corrections that may be necessary.

8. If the brake's adjustment was affected (see step 1 above), tension the cable and adjust the brake.

Tighten Handlebars in Stem

The connection between the handlebars and the stem should also be firm, so the handlebars don't twist out of their proper orientation. To do this, simply tighten the bolts that clamp the stem collar around the bars, using a 5 or 6 mm Allen key. On older models, use a 12 mm wrench to tighten the nut.

Remove and Install Handlebars and Stem Together

This work has to be done in order to work on the headset or to replace the front fork. How the handlebars and the stem are replaced individually will be shown in a subsequent procedure.

Tools and equipment:
• 5–6 mm Allen key (on older bikes 12 mm wrench)
• rag
• grease
• mallet or hammer (sometimes)

Removal procedure:

1. Loosen and detach brake and gear cables from the levers on the handlebars.

2. Loosen the expander bolt by 3–4 turns, or until the stem is loose.

3. If the stem won't come loose, unscrew the expander bolt two more turns, lift the wheel off the ground, holding the bike by the handlebars, then tap on the expander bolt with the mallet, after which it will usually come loose. If it doesn't, apply some spray lubricant or penetrating oil between the stem and the collar or locknut at the top of the headset and try again.

4. Remove the handlebars complete with the stem.

Installation procedure:

1. Clean the stem and the inside of the steerer tube with a clean rag, and then put some grease on the wedge (or the cone) and the part of the stem that will go inside the steerer tube, in order to prevent rust and to ease subsequent adjustment or replacement.

2. Tighten the expander bolt so far that the wedge is correctly

Replacing handlebars complete with stem.

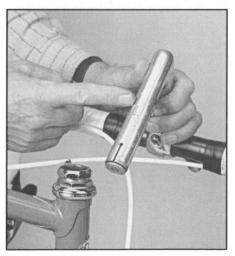

aligned, and snug up to the stem's slanted end, still allowing free movement of the stem in the steerer tube.

3. If a cone-shape device is used instead of a wedge, align the ribs on the cone with the slots in the end of the stem.

4. Install the stem and position it in the correct orientation, but make sure it is not so high that the maximum height mark engraved on the stem protrudes above the headset locknut, so it is clamped in securely.

5. Straddle the front wheel, keeping it straight relative to the bike's frame, and put the handlebars in the required position as regards height and orientation, holding them steady with one hand.

6. Still holding the handlebars firmly in place, tighten the expander bolt.

7. Verify whether the handlebars are now in the right position, and

Loosening binder bolt in stem clamp.

make any corrections that may be necessary.

8. If the brake's adjustment was affected (see step 1 above), tension the cable and adjust the brake as described in Chapter 9.

Replace Handlebars or Stem Separately

This must be done when the handlebars are seriously damaged or when you want to install another size or model of either the stem or the handlebars. When replacing either, first check whether the handlebars and the stem have matching diameters. Generally, it is easiest to do this without first removing the stem from the bike, so that you can use the bike for leverage.

Tools and equipment:
• 3–6 mm Allen keys (on older bikes, 12 mm wrench)
• medium-sized and large screwdrivers

Removal procedure:

1. Remove any components installed on the handlebars, e.g. handlebar tape or handgrips, brake levers, gear shifters — after first releasing tension in the cables.

2. Loosen and remove the bolt(s) that clamp the stem collar around the handlebars.

3. Using the big screwdriver, spread open the collar and pull the thicker section of the handlebars out of the collar. If the stem has a spreader screw, screw it in to open up the collar until it is open wide enough to clear the handlebars.

4. Twist the handlebars in such a way as to find the most favorable position to release them from the stem.

Installation procedure:

1. Open up the handlebars as described in step 3 above.

2. Push the handlebars through the collar, twisting if necessary, until the thicker section is reached, then open up the collar with the big screwdriver or, on models with a spreader screw, by screwing it in using the small Allen key.

3. Push the handlebars into the correct position.

4. Install the clamping bolts and tighten them until the bars are just gripped but not tight.

5. Adjust the handlebars to the exact position desired and hold them there firmly while tightening the bolts. On a model with a spreader

Replacing the handlebars separate from the stem.

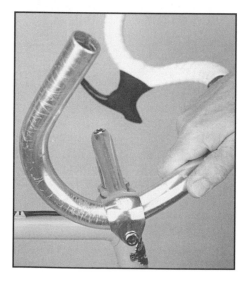

bolt, remember to slacken it off before attempting to tighten the clamping bolts.

6. Install all the components required on the handlebars.

7. Check the position and alignment again, making any adjustments that may be necessary.

8. Finally, on models with a spreader screw, tighten it just enough so it won't get lost.

Replace Handlebar Tape

Drop handlebars are usually covered with handlebar tape, which has to be replaced when it gets uncomfortable or unsightly owing to wear or damage. You will also have to rewrap it if it has been removed in order to replace a brake lever or the stem. Since brake cables are often routed along the bars, you will have to rewrap when replacing an outer cable. Choose either non-adhesive cork, plastic or rag tape, or tape with a narrow adhesive backing strip. At least one roll of tape is needed for each side. Nowadays, most sets of handlebar tape come with two short pre-cut pieces to be used at the brake hoods where the handlebars are bare.

Procedure:

1. Remove the old handlebar tape after loosening the handlebar end plugs. Adhesive tape may have to be cut, after which it is advisable to clean the adhesive off with methylated spirit. Lift the rubber brake hoods off the levers so they clear the handlebars and place the short sections of tape there.

2. Adhesive tape is wound starting from a point about 7.5 cm (3 in.) from the center, working towards the ends. Overlap each layer generously with the preceding one and wrap in an X-pattern around the brake lever attachments.

3. Non-adhesive tape is wound start-ing from the ends, after tucking a piece inside. Work towards the center, and overlap as described above for adhesive tape. Fasten the ends by wrapping some ad-hesive tape around them.

4. Install the end plugs, and tighten them with a screwdriver if they are of the variety with an ex-pander screw in the end.

Remove and Replace Handgrips

On a mountain bike or a roadster, you may want to replace the hand-grips with a more comfortable type. You will also have to remove them when replacing the bars without the stem.

Tools and equipment:
• small screwdriver
• rag
• dishwashing liquid

• hot water
• special adhesive or hairspray

Procedure:

1. Lift the ends of the grips off the handlebars a little with the small screwdriver and introduce some dishwashing liquid if they won't come off easily.

2. Before reinstalling the handgrips, remove all traces of dishwashing liquid, so they won't slide off.

3. To install, dip the handgrips in hot water before forcing them over the handlebars, or use the adhesive that is supplied with some grips— it not only holds them in place once installed, it also helps them slip on when it is first applied.

Bar-Ends and Extensions

Many mountain bike riders feel the regular mountain bike handlebars are too restrictive and decide to in-stall bar ends (also called "bull horns") at the ends. Internally clamped models have a wedge and an expander bolt that works just like the device that holds the stem in the steerer tube. Externally clamped models have a split collar just like a

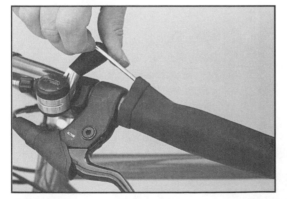

Removal of handgrips.. If they don't come off this way, squirt in some dishwashing liquid as a lubricant. When installing them, you can use hairspray to ease installation and keep them firmly.

handlebar stem. First cut back the ends of the handgrips and then install the bar ends by tightening the Allen bolt that pulls the wedge inside the handlebar end. You must tighten them firmly enough so they don't slip under load. Get the size that matches the diameter of your handlebars, and check to make sure your handlebars are strong enough for the use of bar-ends — some of the lightest handlebars are not.

On road bikes, special clamp-on extensions can be used that extend forward from the drop handlebars, allowing a very low position for time-trial racing. These extensions are clamped on around the straight section of the regular handlebars.

Shorten Straight Handlebars

Some mountain bikes are still supplied with excessively wide handlebars. If you are not unusually big, you may want to shorten them to about 55 cm (22 in.) but certainly no more than 60 cm (24 in.) total width. This can be done once they are installed, using either a pipe-cutter (from a plumbing supply shop) or a hacksaw. Be careful when riding the bike until you get used to the new

situation, because this changes the bike's handling characteristics.

Tools and equipment:
• pipe cutter or hacksaw
• adhesive tape (e.g. handlebar tape)
• file

Procedure:

1. Remove handgrips and measure off the same distance on both sides, marking the location to be cut.

2. If you use a hacksaw, wind some adhesive tape around the bars at the desired cut location to use as a guide to make sure you cut them straight.

3. Stand in such a position that you can cut perfectly square, and preferably get someone else to hold bike and handlebars firmly.

4. File the rough edge smooth.

5. Reinstall all components that were removed from the handlebars.

The Headset

The headset forms the link between the steering system and the frame. It

Bar-ends, as used on many mountain bikes. These are clamped around the ends of the handlebars with a binder bolt reached from below. Other models fit inside the ends of the handlebars and are held with an expander bolt.

consists of two sets of ball bearings installed at either end of the head tube. The lower headset bearing sits between the fork crown and the bottom of the head tube. The upper headset bearing is adjustable, with the adjusting parts screwed onto the top end of the fork's steerer tube. The handlebar stem projects from the locknut at the top of the upper headset bearing.

Although most road bike headsets are made to the same dimensions and are mutually interchangeable, the matter is complicated on mountain bikes since the introduction of various oversize headsets. The headset's nominal size is referenced by the outside diameter of the steerer tube. Work on oversize headsets calls for special tools.

Adjust Headset

If the steering is rough or loose first try to solve the problem by adjusting

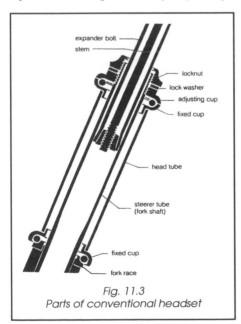

Fig. 11.3
Parts of conventional headset

the headset bearings. If this does not do the trick, the bearing cups may well have been damaged — either as a result of impact from the bearing balls or due to overtightening. In that case, proceed to the next procedure to overhaul the headset.

Tools and equipment:
• headset wrenches (or 10- or 12-inch crescent wrench)

Procedure:

1. Loosen the collar or locknut on the upper headset bearing by about one turn if there is no serrated ring under it — enough to free the latter if there is. If there is a grub screw to clamp the locknut down, undo it first.

2. Lift the washer under this nut enough to release the underlying part, which is the adjustable bearing cup.

3. Tighten or loosen the adjustable bearing cup by turning it by about ⅛ of a turn in the appropriate direction if the bearing is too loose or too tight. Usually this can be done by hand without a wrench.

4. Hold the adjustable bearing cup perfectly still by facing the bike with the front wheel firmly clamped between your legs, and holding the cup with the headset wrench.

5. Put the washer in place and tighten the locknut, while restraining the adjustable cup.

6. Check to make sure the adjustment is correct; readjust if necessary, following the same procedure.

7. On models with a grub screw to clamp the locknut down, tighten it, so the locknut won't come loose accidentally.

Note:

To keep track of your adjustment, it is a good idea to mark the adjustable cup and the head tube with a vertical line showing the original alignment of the two. Then turn the adjustable cup 6 mm (¼ in.) to the right, clockwise, looking down on it from the top, if you want to tighten the headset (or to the left, counterclockwise, if you want to loosen it).

Overhaul Headset

If adjusting does not solve your problem, the headset bearings must be dismantled, and individual parts cleaned, inspected and lubricated — or, if they are damaged, replaced. The

same procedures are followed when either the headset or the fork is replaced. Before doing this work, remove the handlebars with the stem as described in the beginning of this chapter. On a bike with cantilever or centerpull brakes, first loosen the front brake cable.

Tools and equipment:
• headset wrenches (or 10- or 12-inch crescent wrenches)
• bearing grease
• rags

Dismantling procedure:

1. Loosen and remove the collar or locknut on top of the headset, after unscrewing a clamp screw (if installed).

2. Remove the lockwasher by lifting it straight off.

3. Unscrew the adjustable bearing cup, while holding the fork to the frame.

Disassembly or adjusting of conventional headset.

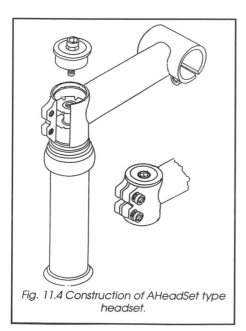

Fig. 11.4 Construction of AHeadSet type headset.

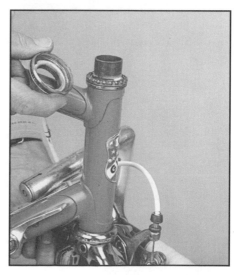

4. Remove the bearing balls, which are usually held in a bearing-ball retainer.

5. Pull the fork out from the frame, also catching the lower bearing balls, again usually held in a retainer. If loose balls are used, make sure you remove all of them and check their size — different diameters are used on different makes and models.

Inspection and overhauling procedure:

1. Inspect all parts for wear, corrosion, grooves, and pitting. Irregular pitting of the bearing races, referred to as brinelling and caused by axial impact, is particularly pernicious. This problem is often caused or aggravated by improper adjustment — that's why I recommend you check and adjust the headset bearings once a month.

2. Replace the entire headset if significant damage is apparent in the cups. Always replace the bearing balls, making sure to count them and buy the correct size, either individually or in a retainer.

3. If the headset bearing races have to be replaced, get the old fixed cups and the fork-crown race removed and new ones installed with special tools at a bike shop.

Note:

Recently, cartridge bearing headset have become more common. On these, the entire bearing unit can be easily replaced, while the parts that

fit in the head tube and the front fork don't wear.

Installation procedure:

1. If the fixed cups and the fork race are serviceable, or once they have been replaced, fill the bearing cups with bearing grease.

2. Hold the frame upside down and embed one of the bearing retainers, or a set of loose bearings, in the grease-filled lower fixed bearing race (which is now facing up). The retainer must be installed in such a way that the bearing balls — not the metal ring — contact the inside of the cup.

3. Hold the fork upside-down and put it through the head tube.

4. Turn the frame the right way round again.

5. Embed the other bearing retainer, or loose bearings, in the grease-filled upper fixed bearing cup.

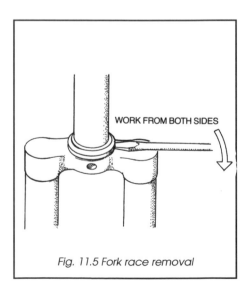

WORK FROM BOTH SIDES

Fig. 11.5 Fork race removal

6. Screw the adjustable bearing cup on the threaded end of the fork's steerer tube by hand.

7. Place the keyed lock washer on top of the adjustable cup with the flat part matching the flat part of the fork's steerer tube, and do the same with any part that may have been installed to serve as a brake cable anchor.

8. Screw the collar or locknut onto the threaded end of the steerer tube, without tightening it completely.

9. Install the front wheel.

10. Adjust the bearings as outlined in the previous description *Adjust Headset*. Take your time for this adjustment, because it can ruin your headset (and impair the bike's handling) if it is too tight or too loose.

11. Center and adjust the stem with the handlebars, and readjust the brake cable if necessary.

12. On models with a clamping screw, screw it in to clamp the locknut tight.

The Front Fork

The front fork consists of a steerer tube (or fork shaft), a fork crown, two fork blades and, at the end of the fork blades, fork-ends or drop-outs. The fork blades are bent forward by a certain distance, referred to as rake.

When the bike hits an unmovable object—whether this be a tree, a curbstone or a rain gutter in the road — the front fork is the most likely part of the bike to be damaged: the

fork blades will get bent back. Other forms of damage are a bent steerer tube, which will be noticed if the steering becomes stiff, a broken steerer tube (there's no way you can fail to notice that, if you survive the accident) or sideways misalignment of the fork blades, which is often the result of careless transportation of the bike. The last problem is avoided by installing an old hub or similar blocking device between the fork-ends when the front wheel is removed from the bike. To verify if the fork is straight, carry out the following alignment check.

Fork Alignment

There are several different ways the fork may be bent, each requiring a different test.

Tools and equipment:
• metal straightedge
• a perfectly level surface
• a perfectly level block, at least 5 cm (2 in.) high and 20 cm (8 in.) long
• callipers

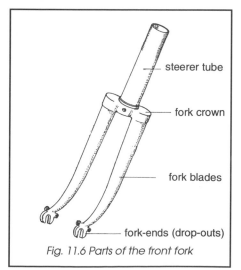

Fig. 11.6 Parts of the front fork

steerer tube

fork crown

fork blades

fork-ends (drop-outs)

Checking Procedure

1. Check with the straightedge whether the upper portion of the fork blades lies in line with the centerline through the fork shaft (if the fork is still in the bike, line up with the centerline of the head tube). If it's not, either the blades or the fork shaft are bent. If the steering operates smoothly, it will be the fork blades, which can often be corrected (see below); otherwise it will be the fork shaft, which will almost certainly require a new fork.

2. To check whether the fork blades are bent unequally, place the fork on the level surface, resting on the fork-ends, and with the upper portion of the blades on the edge, which must be exactly perpendicular to the fork. If the fork does not rest on all four points, it is misaligned. Note which way it is misaligned by drawing an arrow on the blade that has to be corrected — see below for straightening procedure.

3. To check whether the distance between the blades is correct, check whether the front hub fits snugly, without having to force the fork blades sideways either in or out. If this test shows any misalignment, the last test (step 4) must also be carried out.

4. To check whether the fork is offset laterally, place the fork on the level block (which in turn is on the level surface) resting on the fork shaft with one blade down. Make sure the blades are exactly vertically above one another, then measure the distance between the lower fork-end and the level surface. Now turn the fork over and do the same check with the other blade down. If the distances are not identical to within 1.5 mm (1/16 in.), the fork blades should be cold-set correspondingly. See the description for fork alignment correction below.

Checking fork blade alignment. These are parallel but slightly out of alignment with the steerer tube.

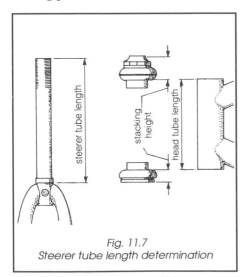

Fig. 11.7
Steerer tube length determination

Alignment Procedure:

As long as the fork is not too severely bent and the steerer tube (fork shaft) is still straight, it will usually be possible to correct misalignment of the fork. This is the same kind of cold setting operation as described for the frame in Chapter 12. Do it carefully, but not without force. Just clamp the steerer tube in a vise, protecting it with two blocks of wood with V-grooves as shown; place a 60 cm (24 in.) long piece of 1½-in. diameter tubing over the blade that is to be corrected, as close as possible to the area with the most serious portion of the bend, and force it in the appropriate direction. After bending, carry out the previously described check again, and correct if necessary. Check to make sure there are no sharp irregular bends or cracks before reinstalling the fork. If the fork-ends are not perfectly parallel or are bent, straighten them out by placing them in. the vice over their entire length or up to the point of their bend, then force the fork over as required to straighten the fork-end.

Inspect and Replace Front Fork

This will be necessary whenever you have had a serious crash or when the bike does not seem to steer the way it should. Generally, a visual check is adequate for the typical kinds of damage possible.

Although it may sometimes be possible to straighten a bent fork, I suggest you replace the entire fork. This will give you a sorely needed margin of safety that may prevent a bad crash later on. Sometimes the fork's steerer tube has to be cut shorter to fit the frame. It is preferable to get that done at the bike shop, since the thread often has to be recut too.

If you decide to do it yourself, screw the locknut on as a guide so you'll cut straight. Be careful not to cut it too short — better to add an

Even if the fork itself is not damaged, the pivot bosses on a mountain bike fork may be, and it still has to be replaced.

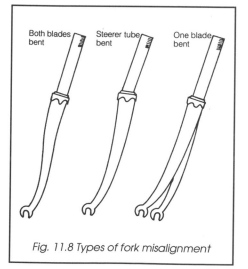

Fig. 11.8 Types of fork misalignment

extra washer or file it down farther than ruin your fork. File any burrs off the end before installing the fork. Before doing this work, remove the handlebars with the stem. On a bike with cantilever or centerpull brake in the front, loosen the brake cable and remove the front wheel.

Tools and equipment:
• 3–6 mm Allen keys
• headset wrenches or 10- or 12- inch crescent wrench

Procedure:

1. Release the front brake cable and remove the entire front brake; then remove the front wheel.

2. Remove the handlebars with the stem.

3. Dismantle the upper headset as outlined in *Overhaul Headset*.

4. Remove the fork, following the same description.

Oil-damped air pressure type suspension fork. On this model, the air pressure can be controlled via the valve shown here.

5. Use the old fork as a reference to buy the new one, taking it to the bike shop with you.

6. Install the fork and reassemble the headset as described under *Overhaul Headset*.

7. Install the handlebars as described above.

8. Install the front brake and hook up the cable.

9. Install the front wheel.

10. Check and adjust all parts affected: headset, stem, handlebars, front brake.

Front Suspension

In recent years, telescoping front forks have become popular for mountain bikes. The number of different versions on the market is too great to do justice to any one of the detailed maintenance instructions.

Perhaps the most important advice is to keep them scrupulously clean, especially near the area where the thinner section telescopes in the thicker section. Any dirt that penetrates is likely to reach the seals (on models with hydraulic dampers) and cause leakage, resulting in inadequate damping. On models without hydraulic damping, penetrating dirt may cause the parts to bind up, resulting in unpredictable behavior.

Regularly check for any apparent looseness or tightness in the suspension and steering functions. If you notice a loss of front end control when riding, that will probably be owing to damage to the fork's mechanism. Refer any work that goes beyond cleaning and adjusting to a

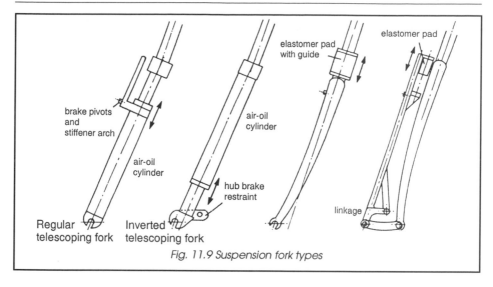

Fig. 11.9 Suspension fork types

bike mechanic familiar with this kind of equipment. Alternatively, you can request the specific maintenance instructions from the manufacturer of the fork.

To install a suspension fork, follow the same procedure as previously described for a rigid fork. When selecting one as a replacement for a rigid fork, make sure you select one with the same steerer tube diameter and length. That's easiest to do when you take the whole bike to the shop so it can be measured by an expert. Once installed, take the bike for a test ride. If the steering feels loose, check over the entire installation again. If you can't figure out yourself what is wrong, take it to the bike shop.

Elastomer Suspension Fork Maintenance

Most of these have a knob or dial with which the frictional damping is adjusted and they can be dismantled to replace the elastomer pads. Always keep your adjustments symmetrical, so both sides of the fork are adjusted the same way. Generally, heavier riders need stiffer pads and more damping than light riders. If the suspension seems too soft, turn the dial clockwise to tighten up on the friction damping; turn counterclockwise to loosen it up. Try out various settings to establish which way seems most comfortable.

To replace the elastomer pads, first take the front wheel out and dismantle the fork blade, which on most models is done from a large screw cap at the top. Take the inner sliding tube out to reveal something that looks like a plunger that is mounted between elastomer pads. The pads will be color coded according to their firmness. Generally the stiffest are white, moderately firm ones are yellow, and the softest ones are red. Select the combination that seems right, considering your weight, riding style and the feel of the forks before modification. It is possible to mix and match, in which case the stiffest ones are used at the ends, the softest ones in the middle. Finally, reassemble the

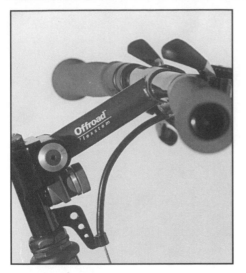

Simple elastomer flexible stem. Preload is adjusting with the round knurled nut.

fork and test-ride it immediately — and make such additional adjustments as may seem appropriate.

Air-Sprung Suspension Fork Maintenance

Of all the "shocks," this type, of which the Rock-Shox are the best known example, is technically the most sophisticated, and consequently also the most sensitive. The pressure is adjusted by changing the gas pressure (either nitrogen or simply air, depending on the make and model in question). Most of the models that use air can be controlled via a simple valve (either like that on a car tire or like the one on a football), using a pump or a compressor with the matching adaptor. The tension is lowered by letting off some air by pushing in the valve pin. Heavy riders, rough terrain and high speeds require higher pressures than lighter riders, less rugged terrain and lower speeds.

These forks are damped by means of a hydraulic shock absorber — a piston with a small hole moving up and down in an oil-filled cylinder. Within the normal range, damping is increased by selecting a higher number, and decreased by selecting a lower number on the dial. If damping is still inadequate, you may replace the oil by a type with a higher viscosity. Although the manufacturers offer supposedly specially formulated oils under their own brand name, this is probably not significantly different from generic oil. The cheapest and e equally effective way is to use automatic transmission fluid (ATF), available from auto part stores, and the higher the number the stiffer will be the damping effect.

Other Suspension Methods

The simplest form of effective suspension is by means of a sprung stem, of which there are several types on the market. In most cases, a coil spring is used, supplemented by elastomer pads to soften the bottoming out. On cheaper models, only an elastomer pad is used as a spring. The most sophisticated coil-spring models have an adjuster to preload the coil spring more or less. In addition, there may be a friction adjustment to increase or decrease the damping effect.

Since this kind of suspension does not affect the steering geometry, as all suspension forks do, it can be retrofitted by the home mechanic to any existing bike — it does not even have to be a mountain bike. Simply follow the instructions for removal and installation of the handlebars and the stem elsewhere in this chapter.

CHAPTER 12

The Frame

Although the frame is the bicycle's major single part, it is fortunately rarely in need of maintenance or repair work. And when something does happen, it is likely to be so serious that the average rider decides to call it a day and perhaps even abandon the bike. Just the same, there are some maintenance aspects of the frame that will be covered here.

Frame Construction

The front part, or main frame, is made up of large-diameter tubes. These are called the top tube, down tube, seat tube and head tube, respectively. The bottom bracket shell is at the frame's lowest point. The rear triangle is built up of double sets of smaller-diameter tubes, called seat stays and chain stays, respectively. Each pair is connected by means of a short bridge piece.

Seat cluster detail of a high-quality road frame

Traditionally, bike frames are constructed with external lugs and brazed-in tubes. More recently many frames have been built without lugs, and the tubes may be either welded, bonded or brazed together. The tubes of brazed frames are always of steel, whereas the other methods may be used with more exotic tubing materials, such as aluminum, titanium and carbon-fiber.

Whether welded, brazed or bonded, one lug is always present:

Bottom bracket detail. on the same lugged frame.

the seat lug. It is split in the back and clamped together to hold the saddle. At the ends where the stays meet there are flat plates, called drop-outs, in which the wheel is installed. The one on the right also contains a threaded eye, to which the derailleur is mounted. Finally, there are a number of small parts, referred to as braze-ons. These range from the pivot bosses for the shift levers on road bikes, or for the mountain, hybrid or touring bike's special can-tilever brakes, to little bosses for the installation of water bottle, luggage carrier, cable guides.

Frame Damage

In the case of a head-on collision, there is a chance of the down tube literally buckling at a point just be-hind the head tube. Left unchecked, this will eventually lead to the frame's collapse, which may prove highly dangerous. It's the kind of damage only a professional frame builder can solve for you — and one that's only worthwhile on an expen-sive frame because the down tube has to be removed and replaced by a new one.

Other kinds of frame damage are less dramatic, though they may be serious enough. A collision, a fall or other forms of abuse may cause the frame to get out of alignment. You can verify this from time to time by trying to line up front and rear wheel, while looking from behind. If it can't be done, either the frame or the front fork is misaligned. The descriptions below show you how to check the frame and what to do about it. Finally, it sometimes hap-pens that one of the drop-outs gets bent. Instructions to establish and cor-rect this problem are also contained below.

The possibilities of aligning and bending are limited to conventional steel frames. Don't try this kind of operation on frames made of aluminum, nor on the lightest

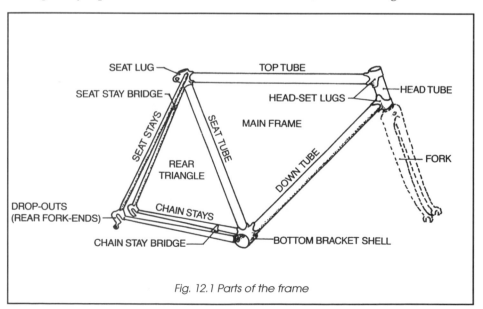

Fig. 12.1 Parts of the frame

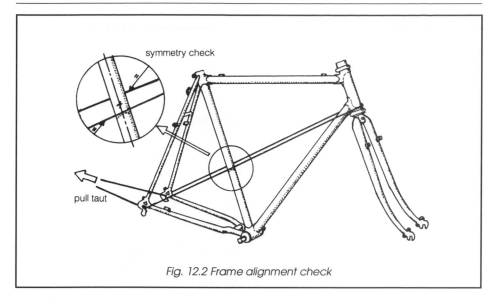

symmetry check

pull taut

Fig. 12.2 Frame alignment check

varieties of steel (such as Reynolds 753, Columbus SLX and Max, or Tange Prestige tubing). And nobody can straighten the new crop of composite and bonded frames — not even an experienced bike mechanic or frame builder.

Frame Alignment Check

In this and the following procedures, all the checks that can be carried out relatively simply will be described in some detail. Always see a bike shop about correcting any damage detected.

Tools and equipment:
• 3 m (10 ft.) of twine
• ruler marked in mm or 32nds

Procedure:

1. Remove the rear wheel from the bike, following the relevant description in Chapter 4.

2. Wrap the twine around the frame, pulling it taut at the drop-outs.

3. Measure the distance between the twine and the seat tube on both sides. If they are not identical (plus or minus perhaps 1 or 2 mm at the most), let a bike mechanic determine whether the frame can be straightened — it's not the kind of job to do yourself.

Drop-out Check

After a fall, the reason for derailleur problems may be that the rear derailleur eye (on the RH rear drop-out) is bent. In other cases, the wheel won't center, even though it seems to be undamaged (as checked in Chapter 4). To establish whether the drop-outs are still straight after a fall or rough transportation, proceed as follows.

Tools and equipment:
• 60 cm (2 ft.) long metal straightedge
• callipers or ruler marked in mm or 32nds

Procedure:

1. Remove the rear wheel from the bike, following the relevant procedure in Chapter 4.

2. Hold the straightedge snug up against the outside of the drop-outs on both sides, holding, but not forcing, the other end near the down tube.

3. Compare the distance of the straightedge from the seat tube on both sides.

4. Measure the distance between the drop-outs and compare it with the sum of the seat tube diameter and the two distances just measured.

5. If the difference is more than 3 mm (1/8 in.), at least one of the drop-outs should be straightened – preferably by a bike mechanic, but you may want to try your hand at it yourself. Usually, you can tell which one is bent.

Note:

Any misalignment noticed in this test should not be corrected by the home mechanic. Consult a competent bike mechanic or a frame builder to correct the problem.

Paint Damage Touch-up

However careful you are, you can't help but scratch up your bike sometimes. At least once a year it will be worthwhile to touch up any nicks and scratches. For a complete description of this work, see Chapter 15. You are warned though, that some frames, specifically those made of exotic materials such as carbon fiber or bonded composite materials, should not be touched with either solvents or paints, since this may weaken them, or at a minimum voids the manufacturer's guarantee.

Frame Straightening

The way bent frames are straightened is politely referred to as cold setting: bending them back straight without heating. That may sound crude, but it's essentially the same method used by professionals, who of course use more sophisticated tools and measuring equipment, although the principle is the same.

Don't try doing this yourself on a sensitive lightweight frame. But if you're not of a nervous nature, you may try doing it yourself, unless your frame is one of the most expensive models, since in that case the risk of doing damage is much greater, due to the very light tube gauge used. We'll assume you have established in the preceding check what exactly is the nature of your problem, and know just how much you have to bend which part in which direction.

Nine times out of ten, the problem with a misaligned frame is caused by the rear triangle (seat and chain stays). It is possible that the seat tube and the head tube do not lie in the same plane, but it's unlikely and hard to correct. Besides, bending the rear triangle may correct adequately to compensate for the effect of this kind of misalignment as well. The thinner tubes of the rear triangle are easier to bend — both unintentionally, causing the problem in the first place, and intentionally, to correct it again. So that's what I'll describe here. No special tools will be required for this job.

Procedure:

1. First establish exactly how far each half of the rear triangle has to be bent out and in which direction, based on both the over-lock-nut dimension of the rear hub and the alignment check described above.

2. Place the frame on a strong table or a similar level area, the rear triangle protruding over the edge. I like to use the front porch, except for the public attention it draws to the crudeness of this operation. Get a friend to stand on the frame at the head tube and the seat tube.

3. Bend the side that's facing up in or out until the correct position has been reached, comparing the distance between the lower and the upper drop-outs before and after bending.

Fig. 12.3 Rear triangle check

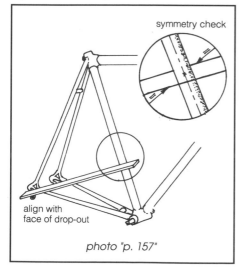

symmetry check

align with
face of drop-out

photo "p. 157"

4. Turn the frame over and do the same with the other rear triangle. When you've finished, the distance between the drop-outs should be identical to the over-locknut width of the rear hub.

5. Carry out the alignment check described above and make any corrections that may be necessary.

Straighten Drop-outs

Drop-outs or fork-ends, as they are called in Britain, should be parallel and straight. Especially the RH drop-out should be checked when the derailleur gearing gives you trouble — if it's bent, correct the drop-out before readjusting the gears. If the drop-outs aren't parallel and straight, as established in the description *Frame Alignment Check* above, they can usually be bent back without doing serious damage (at least on most steel frames) quite easily.

The professional way is to use a special tool that screws into the derailleur eye or hooks around the entire drop-out. However it can often be done without a special tool: Place a crooked drop-out in the jaws of the vise over its entire length and, using the frame for leverage, bend it back into shape.

If you don't have a vise, let someone else hold the frame and, using a big crescent wrench, set for the exact thickness of the drop-out, bend the thing back. If the wrench give insufficient leverage, you may fit a piece of tube (water pipe or whatever) over the top of the handle. If the drop-out itself is not straight, use two wrenches or a wrench and a vise, one on either side of the bend, to correct

Drop-out straightening using special but simple alignment tools. Bend until the cylindrical facings of the two sides of the tool are level and aligned.

the situation. Always check again when you've finished and make any corrections that may be called for. If noticeable cracks have developed, or if the drop-out is seriously bent out, it may be necessary to have the entire drop-out replaced: go and see a bike mechanic about a job like that.

Straighten Derailleur Eye

One of the causes for rear derailleur problems is a bent derailleur eye on the RH drop-out. This can only be corrected if you use a special tool. If you try to do this by clamping the derailleur eye in the vise and then twist it, or use a crescent wrench, the screw thread will get deformed so the derailleur no longer goes on straight.

CHAPTER 13

Saddle and Seatpost

Although these are not amongst the most trouble-prone components on the modern bicycle, they do justify some attention. The jobs described here will be adjustment of the position of the saddle (also called seat), replacement of saddle and seatpost and any maintenance needed on a leather saddle. The Hite-Rite adjusting aid, installed on many top-quality mountain bikes, is described in Chapter 14, which deals with accessories.

On the mountain bike, the binder bolt usually takes the form of a quick-release mechanism. The saddle position should be adjusted whenever the bike is set up for another rider or when the position is uncomfortably high or low.

Adjust Saddle Height

In this and the following descriptions, we shall merely explain how the actual adjustment operations are carried out, assuming you know how high you want it to be.

Tools and Equipment:
• 3–5 mm Allen key
• 6 inch crescent wrench
• grease
• rag

Procedure:

1. Undo the binder bolt or, on a mountain bike, flip the lever of the

Mountain bike saddle detail.

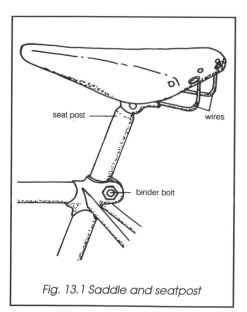

Fig. 13.1 Saddle and seatpost

quick-release binder bolt to the open position in order to loosen the seatpost.

2. The seatpost, with the saddle still attached, should now be free to move up and down. If it is not, undo the bolt further, or on a mountain bike hold the QR lever and unscrew the thumb nut on the other side by about one turn. If it still isn't free, apply some penetrating oil between the seatpost and the seat lug, wait a minute or two and try again, if necessary using the saddle to twist the seatpost relative to the frame.

3. Place the saddle in the desired position. If penetrating oil was needed, first remove it, then clean the seatpost and the interior of the seat tube and apply some grease to the outside of the seat pillar.

4. Hold the saddle at the correct height, and align it perfectly straight forward. Tighten the binder bolt or flip the quick-release lever to the closed position.

5. On a model with quick-release, check whether the saddle is now installed firmly. If not, loosen the quick-release lever, tighten the thumb nut perhaps one turn, and try again.

6. Try out and readjust if necessary until the position is satisfactory.

Note:

If you have a mountain bike with a Hite-Rite spring adjuster, apply just enough downward force on the saddle to achieve the desired position when adjusting. If the range of the Hite-Rite is incorrect for the required

saddle position, undo the clamp around the seatpost and attach it higher or lower as required. Refer to Chapter 14 for additional details.

Adjust Saddle Angle and Position

Generally, both these adjustments are carried out with the bolts that hold the saddle to the seatpost. These can be reached from under the saddle, except on some special seat pillars.

Tools and equipment:
• 3–5 mm Allen key
• 6-inch crescent wrench

Procedure:

1. If the saddle must be moved forward or backward, loosen both bolts by about one or two turns each.

2. Holding the clip on top of the seatpost with one hand and the saddle

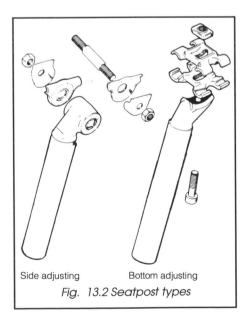

Side adjusting   Bottom adjusting

Fig. 13.2 Seatpost types

with the other, move the latter to the correct position.

3. If the saddle has to be merely tipped, the front raised or lowered relative to the rear portion, loosen the nuts, and then move the saddle as required.

4. Holding the saddle in the correct position, tighten the bolts, making sure it does not move while doing so.

5. Check and readjust if necessary.

Replace Saddle and Seatpost

It is usually easier to remove the combination of saddle and seatpost than to remove the saddle alone. This is also the first step in removing the seatpost.

Removal of the seatpost. On mountain bikes, merely twist the quick-release lever of the binder bolt.

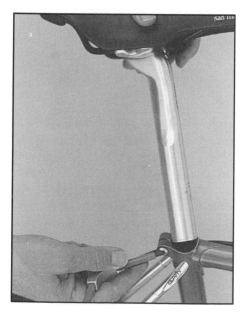

Tools and Equipment:
• 6 inch crescent wrench
• 3–5 mm Allen key

Removal Procedure:

1. Loosen the binder bolt or the quick-release lever until the seatpost can be moved up or down freely, as described under *Adjust Saddle Height*.

2. Pull out the seatpost with the saddle.

Installation Procedure:

1. Clean the outside of the seatpost and the inside of the seat tube, than smear grease on the seatpost to prevent corrosion and to ease subsequent adjustments.

2. Install the seatpost with the saddle fitted and adjust it to the correct height.

3. If you are installing the seatpost with a Hite-Rite, clamp it around the seatpost when it is perfectly aligned and at the maximum height you will ever want the saddle to be.

4. Tighten the quick-release binder bolt as described under *Adjust Saddle Height*.

Notes:

1. Whenever readjusting the seat or installing the seatpost, make sure 65 mm (2½ in.) is clamped in the seat tube.

2. If your bike has a conventional tubular two-piece seatpost, the adjusting mechanism will be contained in a separate clip that connects the saddle to the seat-

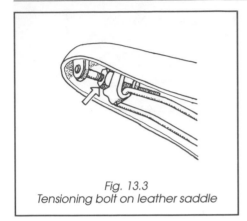

Fig. 13.3
Tensioning bolt on leather saddle

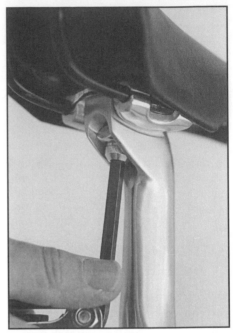

Right: Adjusting the saddle tilt on an adjustable one-piece seatpost.

post. Usually, the bolt only needs to be loosened on one side.

Maintenance of Leather Saddle

If you use a real leather saddle (as opposed to the usual nylon one with a thin leather cover), make sure it does not get wet. Wrap a plastic bag around the saddle when transporting the bike or leaving it outside when there is the slightest chance of rain. If it does get wet, don't sit on it until it is thoroughly dried out, since otherwise it will deform permanently. To keep it water resistant and slightly flexible, treat it with leather treatment such as Brooks Proofide at least twice a year.

Adjust the tension of a leather saddle no more than once a year and only when it is noticeably sagged, tightening the tensioning bolt with the saddle manufacturer's special wrench (regular wrenches don't fit in such a tight spot) — perhaps one turn at the most. Don't overdo this adjustment, since it often causes the saddle to be pulled into an uncomfortable shape.

Even for a sagging cover there is a cure. Drill 4 holes near the middle of each side of the cover, about 8 mm 5/16 in.), and then tie the two sides up the way you might tie your shoelaces. Distribute the tension in such a way that the saddle cover's shape comes as close as possible to the original shape.

Install Sprung Leather Saddle

The most comfortable leather saddles, such as the Brooks ATB Conquest, have double wires and coil springs. To fit this kind of saddle on an adjustable seatpost, you will have to either install the matching model or use a special adaptor between the wires in the saddle. Place the adaptor on the saddle's two pairs of wires and between the seatpost's main part and its clip, then tighten the bolts and adjust the saddle as described elsewhere in this chapter.

CHAPTER 14

Accessories

In the U.S., most bikes are generally ridden with no more than the essential equipment. However, several accessories can be added to most bare-bones bikes, some of them adding significantly to the bike's utility value. In fact, some accessories can be considered essential if you really want to enjoy the full use of your bike.

This chapter will briefly describe how to install and maintain the most useful accessories. We'll cover the following accessories:

- ☐ lock
- ☐ pump
- ☐ seat adjuster
- ☐ toe-clips
- ☐ lighting equipment
- ☐ luggage racks
- ☐ fenders
- ☐ chainguard
- ☐ kickstand
- ☐ cycle computer

The Lock

Whether you use a U-lock or a padlock with a separate chain or cable, you can keep it working with minimum maintenance. Put a drop of oil on the key and on the shackle that enters the lock and open and close it.

The Pump

At home, a big stand pump with hose connector and an integrated pressure gauge is most useful for fast

Simple accessories. Left: Lubricating a U-lock. Right: The workings of a pump head.

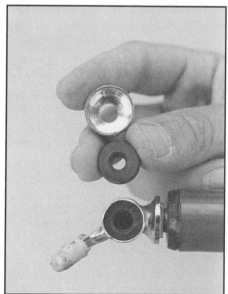

and controlled tire inflation. On the bike, a smaller model will be needed. In addition to the standard versions intended for road bikes, there are special mountain bike pumps available. These have a larger diameter than the models intended for road bikes, allowing you to pump more air with each stroke of the pump, though at a slightly lower pressure. Recently, CO_2 gas inflators have become popular, but they are more hassle than they are worth. Whatever type you use, get a pump with the kind of head or hose connector to match the valves on your bike's tires. If you have to maintain bikes with different types of valves, buy an adaptor nipple to convert from one to the other.

Pump Maintenance

If the pump doesn't work properly, the leak is usually at the head of the pump (the part that is put on the valve) or at the plunger inside the pump. On some pumps, the head can be replaced.

Tools and equipment:
- screwdriver
- lubricant

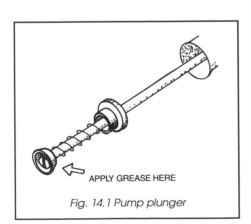

APPLY GREASE HERE

Fig. 14.1 Pump plunger

Procedure:

1. Tighten the screwed bushing that holds down the rubber sealing washer, or grommet, in the head of the pump.

2. If this doesn't solve the problem, unscrew it and check the grommet, replacing it if necessary (inflexible, cut, frayed or enlarged hole); then screw the bushing back on.

3. If still no luck, unscrew the other end of the pump and check the condition of the leather or plastic plunger washer. If it is no longer flexible, impregnate it with any kind of vegetable or animal fat and make sure it is screwed down tight. If necessary replace the plunger washer.

Install Seat Adjuster (Hite-Rite)

For off-road riding, the Hite-Rite is a useful device for mountain bikes which allows you to adjust your seat while riding the bike.

Tools and equipment:
- 6 mm crescent wrench
- screwdriver

Removal procedure:

1. Loosen the clamp that holds it around the seatpost.

2. Remove the saddle with the seatpost.

3. Remove the quick-release binder bolt, by unscrewing the thumbnut all the way.

4. Pull the Hite-Rite off the seat lug's eye bolt.

Installation procedure:

1. Place the lower clip in position at the seat lug's eye bolt.

2. Install the quick-release binder bolt, holding the Hite-Rite in the correct position with the eye between the seat lug eye and the thumbnut.

3. Loosely install the seatpost with the saddle.

4. Tighten the Hite-Rite clamp around the seatpost when the seat is as high as you'll ever want it to be.

5. Complete installation and adjustment of the seatpost and the saddle.

6. Check to make sure the seatpost can be adjusted over the desired range and make any corrections necessary.

Installing a Hite-Rite mountain bike seat adjusting spring.

Toeclips

Most road bikes, and many mountain bikes, are equipped with toe-clips, although they are beginning to make way for clipless pedals. In addition to the conventional toeclips with a strap wrapped around the shoe, there are the short metal strapless clips and, for mountain bike use, plastic strapless ones, as well as simple heavy-duty straps. The latter types merely act to stop the foot from slipping off the pedal, without locking it in there completely. Like the other type, they are installed on the pedal with a set of small screws with nuts to lock them in place. Just make sure they are put on pointing forward (the holes on the other side of the pedal are intended to hold pedal reflectors).

Lighting Equipment

For night-time riding on city streets, almost any light will do. However, under off-road conditions, no single light seems to be bright enough. In fact out in the open off-road terrain, a full moon will serve you better than any light you can buy — if only there were one every night. However, for cycling on roads and reasonably surfaced paths, adequate lighting is available and essential.

Although brighter lights can be obtained with separate rechargeable battery units, the simplest acceptable lights are powered by at least two D-cells (the large cylindrical ones) each.

Battery light installation:

This has to be very general advice, since there are so many makes and models, all differing in detail.

Tools and equipment:
- 6 mm crescent wrench
- 3–5 mm Allen keys
- small screwdriver

Procedure:

Get the appropriate mounting hardware and install the lights in such a way that they do not protrude beyond the bike more than necessary. The highest mounting position is generally the best, since it throws fewer confusing shadows and is more readily visible to others.

A really big reflector mounted rather low is at least as visible as even the best rear light to all other road users who have lighting themselves and who could endanger you from behind.

Battery light maintenance

This too has to be very general advice, but universally valid for all battery systems.

Tools and equipment:
- spare batteries
- spare bulb
- sandpaper
- battery terminal grease

Procedure:

1. Usually, when a battery light lets you down, it's a matter of a dead or dying battery. Always check that first, by trying the light with other batteries installed.

2. If that does not solve the problem, check whether the bulb is screwed in and contacts the terminal firmly. Scrape the contacts of bulb, battery and terminal to remove dirt or corrosion.

3. If still no luck, check the bulb and replace it if the filament is broken.

4. To prevent corrosion of the contacts, lightly coat the terminals of battery, bulb, switch and any other parts that carry electricity with battery terminal grease.

Batteries

The batteries are a special problem for all forms of battery lighting. Normal dry cell batteries have an output characteristic that is highly life-dependent: when new, the output is about 1.5 V per cell, which gradually falls to an average of 1.2 V, eventually dwindling to nothing. Consequently, the light is bright at first, settles at an average value for some time and then drops off further.

Gaining access to a battery light to check the connections or to replace either the bulb or the batteries.

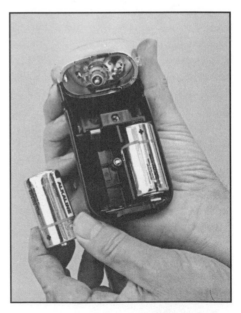

The output of a new battery provides a light that is twice as bright as the average value, while in the end it gives off only a tiny fraction of the average. Bulbs are selected to give the rated output at the average value of 1.2 V per cell (thus, a bulb for a two-cell unit should be rated at 2.4 V, rather than 3 V, as would be suggested by the fact that the cells are quoted as providing 1.5 V each).

Rechargeable batteries are available in the form of nickel-cadmium (NiCad) cells that are fully interchangeable with regular dry cells, or as lead-acid gel batteries suitable only for separate mounting. Both models have entirely different characteristics. The output of a NiCad cell stays relatively constant at 1.2 V and the light remains almost equally bright up to the (shorter) overall charge life, but suddenly dims without warning. This is one reason to carry fully charged spares if you use NiCads. The correct way to maintain NiCad batteries is to run them down completely before recharging them. If they are recharged before they are fully drained, they will soon lose their ability to hold a charge. If this happens, they can usually be revitalized by fully charging and discharging them five times. They have a limited shelf life and should be depleted and recharged at least once a month — and discarded when they fail to hold their charge for a week.

The other form of relatively common rechargeable battery is the lead-acid gel type. These are not available in sizes and shapes that are interchangeable with regular dry cells. They do hold more charge and can be recharged before they are fully run down — in fact, they should never be completely discharged. Consequently, this is best when used as a central battery wired up to separate light units.

Generator Lighting

Generator, or dynamo, lights have the advantage that they are always available for instant use, even if you did not anticipate needing a light — if you give them the little maintenance they need. If they don't work, a systematic approach will usually bring them back to life in little time.

Repair procedure:

When a generator system fails, it is only possible to establish what went wrong if you follow a very systematic approach. After all, this system comprises a large number of mutually connected components. But don't let system rule over logic. Ask yourself what is the most likely cause

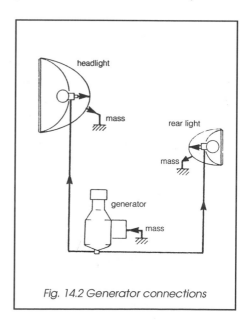

Fig. 14.2 Generator connections

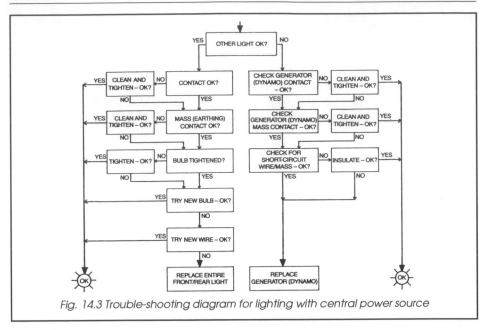

Fig. 14.3 Trouble-shooting diagram for lighting with central power source

under the given circumstances. Thus, when it is raining or snowing, generator slip is more likely to be the cause than in dry weather — so that is the point to start: make sure the generator is aligned properly and increase contact pressure by bending the attachment to bring it closer to the tire.

Reflectors

There are a few points to consider in the selection and maintenance of reflectors. In the first place, bigger is better: larger reflectors are more visible than smaller ones, all else being equal. Secondly, lighter colored reflectors are more visible than darker ones. Amber reflects about twice as much light as red.

As for maintenance, reflectors only do their job properly when they are kept clean: wash them regularly with plenty of water. However, if water should leak inside the reflector, it condenses on the inside, making

the reflector virtually blind. For this reason, a cracked or broken reflector should be replaced immediately. To check a reflector's operation, aim a light at it from a distance of 10 m (33 ft.), observing from a point close to the light source whether the reflector appears to light up brightly.

Luggage Racks

The granddaddy of all modern luggage racks (or carriers, as the British call them) is Jim Blackburn's welded aluminum model, and this is still the favorite of many riders, even if the competition offers significantly cheaper racks that look quite similar.

In the front, use only the so-called *low-rider* variety which allows luggage to be carried where it least interferes with steering and bike handling — centered on the steering axis, just behind the front wheel axle. Unfortunately, they do make it hard to transport the bike on most roof racks.

Luggage rack installation:

Generally, all luggage racks are attached to bosses welded or brazed onto the bike's frame and front fork.

If your bike does not have the requisite bosses, a clip can be used, providing you first wrap the frame or fork tube where you will mount this clip with a large rubber patch, stuck down with rubber solution just as you would do for a flat tire. This protects the paint and prevents slipping of the clip under the effect of load and vibrations.

Fenders

Generally, fenders, or mudguards, are not used on modern road bikes and mountain bikes. However, if you ride in rainy weather or on wet roads or trails, they are essential. Several models are available, the widest and the longest ones being the most effective. Short clip-on fenders don't usually do the trick. In very heavy

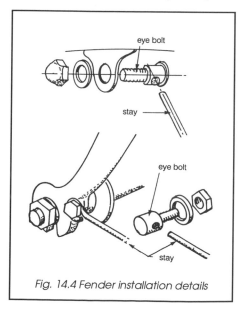

Fig. 14.4 Fender installation details

mud, especially on modern mountain bikes with their limited wheel clearances, fenders can be more trouble than they are worth, since the mud builds up between wheel and fender, soon rendering the former nearly immobile.

Fender installation:

The stays with which the fenders are attached to the eyelets at the dropouts and the clips are bolted through a hole in the fork crown or in the bridge connecting the seat stays. If you want to make the fenders easily removable, use home-made wing-bolts, made by soldering a washer in the (widened) saw cut of a slotted-head screw.

To adjust the position of the fenders, the stays are merely clamped at a different point. Cut off any excess length, so there are no dangerous protrusions on the bike. If the stays are installed inside the clips at the fender, as required in some markets as a safety feature, they must be cut to the right length first.

Chainguard

Simple bikes are often equipped with a protective guard around the chain, which on some models covers the entire drivetrain. After some use, they tend to bend and twist and then rub against the chain, the crank or the chainrings. Don't just try to twist it while on the bike, because that never seems to have the desired result. Instead, first establish which part needs to be bent which way, then remove it from the bike and bend the attachment clips as appropriate. Check and tighten the attachment bolts once a month.

Kickstand

This device, called prop stand in the U.K., is usually only used on simple bicycles. Although few are any good, some models work better than others. The Japanese model that is attached on the rear stays close to the rear wheel axle is much more effective than the more common type that is attached just behind the bottom bracket. Besides, it does not get in the way while wheeling the bike backwards, as the conventional kickstand does.

Another interesting model is the two-legged version. Its advantage is that the bicycle can be balanced on it so that it does not lean over. With this model, either the rear wheel or the front wheel can be raised off the ground to work on the bike. The same maintenance purpose can be achieved by means of a $7 display stand — nothing to install on the bike, but very handy to have at home.

Bicycle Computer

Today, this is about the most common bicycle accessory, and these things are getting both cleverer and smaller every year. Select one that has the minimum number of knobs consistent with the functions you desire. Follow the manufacturer's instructions for installation, calibration and maintenance.

Generally, it must be calibrated for the wheel size, measured accurately between the road and the wheel axle of the loaded bike. Look for a model that is advertised as being

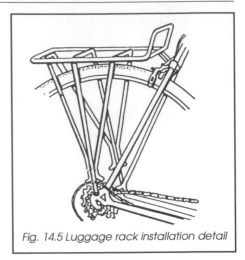

Fig. 14.5 Luggage rack installation detail

waterproof and comes with a guarantee to back up this claim. If it is not, put a plastic bag over it in the rain and always take it off the bike when transporting it.

General Accessory Installation and Maintenance

The following simple rules will help you keep any other accessories on the bike in working order – or at least will prevent their interference with safe operation of the bike.

☐ Attachment must be at a minimum of two points, preferably off-set relative to one another.

☐ If it comes loose, don't just retighten it, but find a better attachment method.

☐ If it gets damaged, remove, repair or replace it immediately.

☐ If it is a moving part, check whether it moves freely without resistance, and lubricate or adjust if not.

CHAPTER 15

Painting a Bicycle

In this chapter I shall give some advice to those readers who want to repaint an old bicycle or touch up paint that is scratched. The best advice to those who are tempted to repaint their entire frame is probably, don't. It is extremely time-consuming and demanding work, which at best produces acceptable results; at the worst it may be a total disaster. Heed the advice in this chapter to improve your chances of success, but don't expect your first attempt to look really satisfactory, though your skills will improve with time and practice.

Do not attempt to repaint any composite or other exotic frame. These frames typically have bonded joints that could be weakened by the solvents used to remove the old paint or contained in the new paint. On some other special frames, the resin in which the fibers are embedded may well be weakened by the use of solvents. In fact, some manufacturers void their frame warranty when the original paint is removed or painted over.

Touch-Up Painting

If my enthusiasm about completely repainting a bike is limited, I do encourage anyone to touch up the paint of his bicycle when it is scratched or chipped. This is simple work that, conscientiously executed, will keep your bike looking good a long time. What you need for the job is a small bottle of matching touch-up paint, a brush, sandpaper, a clean rag and paint thinner or turpentine. The best time to buy matching touch-up paint is when you buy the bike, since manufacturers often revise their color schemes and rarely are eager to supp-

Painting a bicycle frame after it has been completely scraped clean, primed, and sanded down to a smooth surface. Wear a mask to protect your lungs. Wear a mask to prevent inhalation of harmful substances, and avoid breathing in solvent fumes.

ly touch-up paint for a bike that was sold a long time ago. This is a good reason to buy a bike from a major manufacturer (who is more likely to supply touch-up paint in the first place) or to choose any one of the colors in which Henry Ford offered his model T, namely black.

The paint thinner must be selected for compatibility with the kind of paint used. For most ordinary paints that means turpentine, but some modern paints should only be used with specific different solvents — read the instructions for the paint. As for the other necessities, the rag must be lint-free and soft, the brush must have fine short bristles, and the sandpaper must be very fine. Do the work whenever you will not need the bike for a couple of days, so the paint has enough time to cure.

Procedure:

1. Clean the bike (or at a minimum the area around the scratch to be treated) before starting the job. Then sandpaper the damaged area to bare metal, removing any rust. To do that, take a small piece of sandpaper, folded into an even smaller pad.

2. Wipe the sanded area clean with a dry rag, then use a clean part of the rag, soaked in solvent, to clean it thoroughly. Wipe once more with a dry part of the rag. This will remove any dirt or grease that might impair adhesion of the paint.

3. Stir the paint thoroughly, mixing the thinner upper layers well with the thicker lower layer of the contents of the can. If the paint was supplied in a spray can, shake the can well, then spray a "puddle" of paint, concentrated in one place in a small receptacle such as a bottle cap.

4. Dip the tip of the brush in the paint and apply only in the area

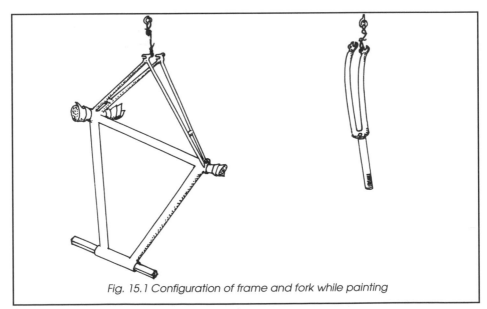

Fig. 15.1 Configuration of frame and fork while painting

where the paint was removed (don't overlap).

5. Clean the brush in solvent. Let the paint cure at least 24 hours before using the bike.

Note:

It is preferable to use two applications of paint: the first one with a primer, which must be compatible with the kind of finish paint used; it must be allowed to cure 24 hours before you apply the finish coat. This will generally improve adhesion and durability.

Repainting a Frame

Before starting this job, be sure you really want to: you'll have to put in a lot of work and you'll be without the bike for several weeks. Your bike shop can probably recommend a paint shop which will do a better job more quickly, at a price that is low considering the amount of work and time you will be investing yourself. If you insist, follow these procedures.

The work can be broken down into several stages: preparation, priming, painting, curing and finishing. Probably the most time consuming part in terms of man-hours is preparation; in terms of total elapsed time, curing takes the longest.

Preparation:

Before you start, remove all parts until you have nothing but a bare frame left. Also remove the bearing cups of the bottom bracket and the head-set as described in Chapters 6 and 11, respectively.

Now the old paint and any rust that has formed must be removed. Do the work in a well ventilated area (a sheltered outside area is probably best). The easiest way is to use a chemical paint stripper, following the instructions on the can and taking care not to get the stuff on your skin and not to breathe in the fumes. Smear it on generously, let it penetrate until the paint is soft and wrinkled, then scrape it off with a putty knife and wash off any remnants, using plenty of water and a hard brush. Repeat for areas where the paint was not completely removed the first time. Wipe dry after rinsing.

Using fine wet-or-dry sandpaper, which you soak in water to remove the embedded particles frequently, remove the last spots of paint. After that, sand the entire frame with dry sandpaper of the same type until you are down to shiny blank metal everywhere. Use strips of sandpaper about 2.5–5 cm (1–2 in.) wide for the

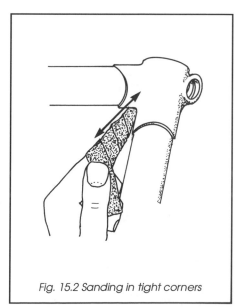

Fig. 15.2 Sanding in tight corners

tubes, narrower strips, wrapped around your finger as shown, to get into all the nooks and crannies. When completed, wipe with a solvent-soaked rag, then with a dry rag. The solvent must be compatible with the particular paint that will be used (check with the store where you buy the paint).

You can save yourself a lot of this work if you can find a shop that will sandblast the frame for you, preferably using fine glass beads, which are less damaging to the metal surface than angular grit or sand. Since especially expensive bicycles are made of thin tubing, excessive sandblasting should be avoided, as it might remove too much metal in critical spots. Wash the sandblasted frame with solvent and then wipe it dry.

Priming:

Select a primer that is of a similar color as the finish coat paint and of a compatible type (i.e. based on the same solvent). If the same color is not available, use a light grey for light shades of paint, a dark grey for dark shades. I usually make two applications of primer, and I thin the paint by adding about 10–20% additional solvent. This will result in a thinner and more even layer of primer.

Between applications, and after the final application, allow the paint to cure at least 24 hours, then sand down to a smooth surface with wet-or-dry sandpaper, washing it out frequently to remove the paint particles that become embedded in the sandpaper. The primer itself can be applied with a brush; use a flat brush, about 2.5 cm (1 in.) wide for the larger tubes, and a narrower

brush for the tight spots. If you can get primer in a spray can, you may choose to use that, provided you practice first, because it is quite tricky to spray an even layer and to cover everywhere. For more advice on spraying, refer to the section *Finish Coat Painting*, below.

Do this and all painting work in a clean, well-ventilated area at temperatures above 10°C (50°F). A sheltered outside area, such as a back porch, is very suitable, provided there is no wind to blow up dust that would ruin the smoothness of the paint.

After completion of the priming and sanding, wash the frame off with a rag, soaked in clean solvent, then dry with a lint-free rag.

Finish Coat Painting:

Although it is possible to use a brush for this work, it will be easier and the result will look better if you use a spray can. Even better would be to use proper spray painting equipment, preferably of the airless variety, which splutters less and gives a smoother coating. Although you can use any spray paint, I have found the ones sold by Schwinn for use on their bicycles particularly suitable, since they seem to cure harder and faster than most regular spray can paints intended for car or household use.

Before you ruin the bike, learn to handle the spray can, trying it out on some other tubular metal construction. Start spraying outside the object to be painted, then move the hand with the spray can evenly over the entire length, finishing beyond the item to be painted. If you were to start spraying while the can is aimed at the bike, the paint would be too thick in those places. Work all around each tube, overlapping each next application until each tube is evenly coated all around, before moving on to the next tube. First do the main tubes, then go on to the rear triangles.

If you do it right, there will be no unpainted areas left in the corners, the lugs and the drop-outs. It will be particularly tricky to touch up such areas later if you don't cover them at the same time as you paint the main tubes, so try to get them covered right away. If you do have to touch up such spots, do it the same way, starting outside the bike, covering the unpainted spot while moving the can along and reversing outside the bike.

While doing the painting, you must not touch the bike. Hang up the frame and the fork as shown in the illustration; use the stick to turn the frame in the appropriate orienta-

Touch-up painting, after sanding down to bare metal only in the area affected.

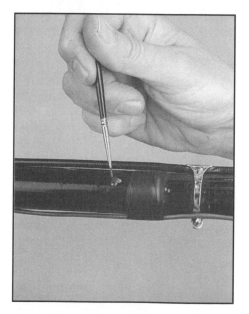

tion. Put old newspaper or a drop cloth under and behind the job, so you don't get paint everywhere. It will be a good idea to wear a mask to avoid breathing in the fumes and paint particles.

There are two entirely different ways of painting, using enamel and lacquer, respectively. Enamel consists of a lot of pigment with a little solvent, which goes on in one or two relatively thick layers. Lacquer is a lot of solvent with relatively little pigment, and requires many more layers, which can be applied within relatively short intervals.

Curing:

Certainly when using enamel, the paint must be allowed to cure very well before the last coat is applied, as it must afterwards, before it is hard enough to handle the bike.

Don't do anything to the bike until the paint is hard, allowing it to cure at least as long as is recommended in the instructions for the paint. Curing must be done in a clean, dry and preferably warm room. When you think the paint is really quite hard, ... wait a few more days before touching it, because even when the surface feels dry, the paint underneath will still be quite soft and easily ruined.

Finishing:

When the paint is finally cured, you may very carefully polish the paint with paint polish, which is a very mild abrasive in liquid solution. Rubbing compound is slightly more abrasive and may only be used on older paint that has been cured several months. After polishing, wash the bike with clean water, wipe it dry and then apply a coat of transparent lacquer. This will provide a harder surface layer and will keep the paint looking bright and shiny longer. Allow the transparent lacquer to harden at least 24 hours before you start reassembling the bike, still taking great care not to scratch the paint when doing so.

If you want certain areas of the bike to be painted in a different color, first paint the smaller sections in the secondary color, overlapping onto the neighboring areas if necessary to cover the proper parts completely. Allow this paint to cure, then cover the part that will remain that color with paper and tape, and paint the rest of the bike, overlapping the taped-off area where necessary.

To apply pin stripes, e.g. highlighting the contours of the lugs, first paint the entire frame and allow to dry completely. Then use a very fine brush with short bristles to apply the contrasting lines.

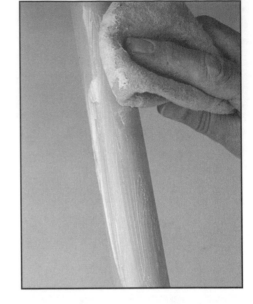

Polishing out fully cured paint using rubbing compound or paint polish.

To apply transfers, wait until the paint is cured, polish and wash the area where the transfer will go, then put on the transfers, following the manufacturer's instruction. If you finish the bike with transparent lacquer, do that after the transfers are in place.

CHAPTER 16

Home-Made Tools and Equipment

In addition to, or in place of, the commercial tools described elsewhere in this book, there are a number of tools and working aids you can easily make yourself. In this section I shall briefly describe a few items that are quite easily made and can be rather handy as substitutes for quite expensive commercial equivalents. Be guided by the drawings, which should speak for themselves without step-by-step building instructions.

Workshop Projects

This first set of projects requires simple woodworking tools and materials that are found almost anywhere or can easily be purchased in any hardware store.

Bike stand:

Raises the bike off the ground while working on it. Either mount it free-standing, clamped between ceiling and floor, or against a wall. You'll need some wooden boards, wood scraps, woodscrews and leather or webbing straps.

Bike hanger:

Another simple device for the same job. You'll need rope, metal wire to bend hooks and eye bolts.

Handlebar support:

The simplest way to work on the bike: merely turn it upside down and rest the handlebars off the ground with this device so it stands steady,

the cables don't get pinched and nothing gets damaged. You'll need wood scraps and woodscrews.

Wheel centering gauge:

This device will allow you to compare the projection of the wheel axle or the locknuts relative to the rim on both sides of a newly built or trued wheel. You'll need a ruler, a plywood board, wood scraps and woodscrews.

Wheel building support:

This simple stand will hold your rim and hub in place while initially building a wheel. You'll need a plywood board, wood scraps and woodscrews.

Lighting test board:

Allows you to test lighting systems with either a central battery or a generator (dynamo). You'll need a 4.5- or 6-volt battery, insulated flexible electric wires, a 6 volt bulb with fixture, a switch, alligator clips (crocodile clips to my British readers), insulated

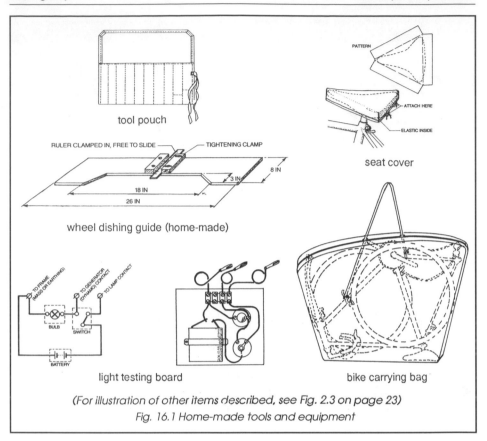

tool pouch

seat cover

wheel dishing guide (home-made)

light testing board

bike carrying bag

(For illustration of other items described, see Fig. 2.3 on page 23)
Fig. 16.1 Home-made tools and equipment

wires, contact strip, wood and metal scraps and woodscrews.

Sewing Projects

This second set of items doesn't even require the use of tools or a workshop: needle and thread is all you'll need for these projects.

Tool pouch:

This is the way to keep your tools organized — at least the few you want to carry with you. Lay out the tools with adequate spaces between them and allow a few spare slots. Sew it from any sturdy piece of scrap fabric and some tape to tie it up.

Saddle cover:

Neater and more durable than an old plastic shopping bag. It is sewn from a small piece of waterproof coated fabric, an elastic band and webbing or tape.

Bicycle carrying bag:

Hidden in this bag, the bike can travel where it otherwise could not. The secret is to attach the carrying straps not to the bag but to the bike frame. Turn the handlebars around, push saddle and handlebars into the frame as far as they will go, and tie the wheels to the frame. Use any light coated fabric, a long zipper and webbing straps.

Back Matter

Appendix:

Gearing Tables

Interchangeability Table

Torque Table

Troubleshooting Guide

Bibliography

Index

Other Titles Available from Bicycle Books

Gearing Table:
Gear Number in Inches

	24	26	28	30	32	34	36	38	39	40	41	42	43	44	45	46	47	48	49	50	51	52	53	
13	48	52	56	60	64	68	72	76	78	80	82	84	86	88	90	92	94	96	98	100	102	104	106	**13**
14	45	48	52	56	60	63	67	70	72	74	76	78	80	82	84	85	87	89	91	93	95	97	98	**14**
15	42	45	49	52	55	59	62	66	68	69	71	73	75	76	78	80	81	83	85	87	88	90	92	**15**
16	39	42	45	49	52	55	58	61	63	65	67	68	70	72	73	75	76	78	80	81	83	85	86	**16**
17	37	40	43	46	49	52	55	58	60	61	63	64	66	67	69	70	72	73	75	76	78	80	81	**17**
18	35	38	40	43	46	49	52	55	56	58	59	61	62	64	65	66	68	69	71	72	74	75	77	**18**
19	33	36	38	41	44	47	49	52	53	55	56	57	59	60	62	63	64	66	67	68	70	71	73	**19**
20	31	34	36	39	42	44	47	49	51	52	53	55	56	57	59	60	61	62	64	65	66	68	69	**20**
21	30	32	35	37	40	42	45	47	48	50	51	52	53	54	56	57	58	59	61	62	63	64	66	**21**
22	28	31	33	35	38	40	43	45	46	47	48	50	51	52	53	54	56	57	58	59	60	61	63	**22**
23	27	29	32	34	36	38	41	43	44	45	46	47	49	50	51	52	53	54	55	57	58	59	60	**23**
24	26	28	30	32	35	37	39	41	42	43	44	45	47	48	49	50	51	52	53	54	55	56	57	**24**
25	25	27	29	31	33	35	37	39	41	42	43	44	45	46	47	48	49	50	51	52	53	54	55	**25**
26	24	26	28	30	32	34	36	38	39	40	41	42	43	44	45	46	47	48	49	50	51	52	53	**26**
27	23	25	27	29	31	33	35	37	38	39	39	40	41	42	43	44	45	46	47	48	49	50	51	**27**
28	22	24	26	28	30	32	33	35	36	37	38	39	40	41	42	43	44	45	46	46	47	48	49	**28**
30	21	23	24	26	28	29	31	33	34	35	36	36	37	38	39	40	41	42	43	44	45	46		**30**
32	20	21	23	24	26	28	29	31	32	33	33	34	35	35	37	37	38	39	40	41	41	42	43	**32**
34	18	20	21	23	24	26	28	29	30	31	31	32	33	33	34	35	36	37	37	38	39	40	41	**34**
38	16	18	19	21	22	23	25	26	27	27	28	29	29	30	31	31	32	32	33	34	35	36	36	**38**
	24	26	28	30	32	34	36	38	39	40	41	42	43	44	45	46	47	48	49	50	51	52	53	

Metric Gearing Table:
Development in meters

	24	26	28	30	32	34	36	38	39	40	41	42	43	44	45	46	47	48	49	50	51	52	53	
13	3.80	4.10	4.50	4.80	5.10	5.40	5.70	6.10	6.20	6.40	6.50	6.70	6.90	7.00	7.20	7.30	7.50	7.70	7.80	8.00	8.10	8.30	8.50	**13**
14	3.60	3.90	4.10	4.40	4.70	5.00	5.30	5.60	5.80	5.90	6.10	6.20	6.40	6.50	6.70	6.80	7.00	7.10	7.30	7.40	7.60	7.70	7.90	**14**
15	3.30	3.60	3.90	4.10	4.40	4.70	5.00	5.30	5.40	5.50	5.70	5.80	5.90	6.10	6.20	6.40	6.50	6.60	6.80	6.90	7.10	7.20	7.30	**15**
16	3.10	3.40	3.60	3.90	4.10	4.40	4.70	4.90	5.10	5.20	5.30	5.40	5.60	5.70	5.80	6.00	6.10	6.20	6.40	6.50	6.60	6.70	6.90	**16**
17	2.90	3.20	3.40	3.70	3.90	4.10	4.40	4.60	4.80	4.90	5.00	5.10	5.20	5.40	5.50	5.60	5.70	5.90	6.00	6.10	6.20	6.30	6.50	**17**
18	2.80	3.00	3.20	3.50	3.70	3.90	4.10	4.40	4.50	4.60	4.70	4.80	5.00	5.10	5.20	5.30	5.40	5.50	5.60	5.80	5.90	6.00	6.10	**18**
19	2.60	2.80	3.10	3.30	3.50	3.70	3.90	4.10	4.30	4.40	4.40	4.50	4.60	4.70	4.80	4.90	5.00	5.10	5.20	5.40	5.50	5.60	5.80	**19**
20	2.50	2.70	2.90	3.10	3.30	3.50	3.70	3.90	4.00	4.10	4.30	4.40	4.50	4.70	4.80	4.90	4.90	5.00	5.10	5.20	5.30	5.40	5.50	**20**
21	2.40	2.60	2.80	3.00	3.20	3.40	3.60	3.80	3.90	4.00	4.10	4.20	4.20	4.30	4.40	4.50	4.60	4.70	4.80	4.90	5.00	5.10	5.15	**21**
22	2.30	2.50	2.60	2.80	3.00	3.20	3.40	3.60	3.70	3.80	3.90	4.00	4.10	4.15	4.20	4.30	4.40	4.50	4.60	4.70	4.80	4.90	4.95	**22**
23	2.20	2.30	2.50	2.70	2.90	3.10	3.20	3.40	3.50	3.60	3.70	3.80	3.90	4.00	4.10	4.15	4.20	4.30	4.40	4.50	4.60	4.70	4.80	**23**
24	2.10	2.20	2.40	2.60	2.80	2.90	3.10	3.30	3.40	3.50	3.50	3.60	3.70	3.80	3.90	4.00	4.10	4.15	4.20	4.30	4.40	4.50	4.60	**24**
25	2.00	2.20	2.30	2.50	2.70	2.80	3.00	3.20	3.25	3.30	3.40	3.50	3.60	3.70	3.70	3.80	3.90	4.00	4.10	4.15	4.20	4.30	4.40	**25**
26	1.90	2.10	2.20	2.40	2.60	2.70	2.90	3.00	3.10	3.20	3.30	3.40	3.40	3.50	3.60	3.70	3.80	3.85	3.90	4.00	4.10	4.15	4.20	**26**
27	1.85	2.00	2.20	2.30	2.50	2.60	2.80	2.90	3.00	3.10	3.20	3.25	3.30	3.40	3.50	3.55	3.60	3.70	3.80	3.80	3.90	4.00	4.10	**27**
28	1.80	1.90	2.10	2.20	2.40	2.50	2.70	2.80	2,90	3.00	3.05	3.10	3.20	3.30	3.35	3.40	3.50	3.60	3.65	3.70	3.80	3.90	3.90	**28**
30	1.70	1.80	1.90	2.10	2.20	2.40	2.50	2.60	2.70	2.80	2.90	2.95	3.00	3.05	3.10	3.20	3.30	3.35	3.40	3.50	3.55	3.60	3.70	**30**
32	1.60	1.70	1.80	1.90	2.10	2.20	2.30	2.50	2.55	2.60	2.70	2.75	2.80	2.90	2.95	3.00	3.05	3.10	3.20	3.25	3.30	3.40	3.45	**32**
34	1.50	1.60	1.70	1.80	2.00	2.10	2.20	2.30	2.40	2.45	2.50	2.60	2.60	2.70	2.75	2.80	2.90	2.95	3.00	3.10	3.15	3.20	3.25	**34**
38	1.40	1.50	1.60	1.70	1.80	2.00	2.10	2.20	2.25	2.30	2.40	2.45	2.50	2.55	2.60	2.70	2.75	2.80	2.85	2.90	2.95	3.00	3.10	**38**
	24	26	28	30	32	34	36	38	39	40	41	42	43	44	45	46	47	48	49	50	51	52	53	

Development

Interchangeability Table

Location	BCI standard (British)	ISO standard (French)	Italian standard	Swiss standard
bottom bracket fixed (RH) side	1.370 x 24tpi (L)	35 x 1mm (R)	1.370 x 24tpi 55°(R)	35 x 24 tpi (R)
bottom bracket adj. (LH) side	1.370 x 24tpi (R)	35 x 1mm (R)	1.370 x 24tpi 55°(R)	35 x 24 tpi (R)
pedal LH side	9⁄16 x 20tpi (L)	14 x 1.25mm (L)	(BCI)	(BCI)
pedal RH side	9⁄16 x 20tpi (R)	14 x 1.25mm (R)	(BCI)	(BCI)
headset (standard)	1.000 x 24 tpi	25 x 1mm	1.000 x 24 tpi 55°	(BCI)
headset (oversize)	not standardized in any system			
freewheel	1.370 x 24 tpi	34.7 x 1 mm	35 x 1mm	(BCI)
derailleur eye	(ISO)	10 x 1mm	10 mm x 26 tpi	(ISO)

Torque Table

Connection	Material	Nm	lb.-ft.
Handlebar stem	any	18–21	12–14
Handlebar binder bolt	any	21–23	14–15
Headset locknut	steel, titanium	37–45	25–30
	aluminum	30–37	20–25
Bottom bracket lockring	steel	30–37	20–25
	aluminum	23–30	15–20
Bottom bracket fixed cup	any	30–37	20–25
Cotterless crank bolt	steel, titanium	37–45	25–30
Chainring attachment	aluminum	6–9	4–6
	steel	9–11	6–7
Pedal attachment	any	45–50	30–33
Saddle binder bolt	steel, titanium	9–12	6–8
Brake mounting bolt	steel, titanium	9–11	6–7
Brake pivot bolt	any	5–7	3–4
Brake lever mounting bolt	any	8–9	5–6
Derailleur mounting bolt	any	9–11	6–7

Problem or Symptom	Possible Cause	Required Correction	See Page
Tiring riding position	1. Incorrect saddle adjustment	Adjust saddle	159
	2. Incorrect handlebar adjustment	Adjust handlebars	138
	3. Incorrect stem extension	Replace stem	140
	4. Incorrect frame size	Replace bike or frame	N/A
High resistance while coasting or pedaling	1. Tire rubs on frame or accessory	Adjust or straighten wheel	37–45
	2. Hub bearings worn or tight	Adjust and lubricate	40
	3. Insufficient tire pressure	Inflate tire	33—35
High resistance while pedaling only	1. Chain dirty, worn or dry	Clean, lubricate, or replace	76–78
	2. Bottom bracket bearings out of adjustment	Adjust, lubricate, overhaul, or replace	67–71
	3. Pedal bearings out of adjustment	Adjust, lubricate, or replace	74–76
	4. Chain or chainring rubs on frame	Straighten or replace, correct chain line	72,77
Rubbing or scraping sounds while pedaling or coasting	1. See above (as for *High resistance while pedaling*)	See above	
Rubbing noise while pedaling	1. Wrong gear selected	Avoid extreme gears	
	2. Front derailleur out of adjustment	Adjust front derailleur	92
	3. Front derailleur under angle	Reposition front derailleur	92
Disturbing noises while pedaling	1. Chainring, crank or pedal loose	Fasten or replace	70–76
	2. Chain dry, dirty or worn	Clean, lubricate, or replace	76–79
	3. Bottom bracket bearing or pedal bearing out of adjustment	Adjust, lubricate, overhaul	68–74
Bike pulls to one side	1. Wheels misaligned	Adjust, center, and align	44–48

Problem	Cause	Remedy	Page
	2. Front fork bent	Replace or straighten	147
	3. Headset damaged	Overhaul or replace	144–145
	4. Frame out of alignment	Straighten or replace	156
Bike vibrates at high speed	1. Wheels misaligned	Adjust or align	37–48
	2. Hub bearings loose	Adjust	40
	3. Headset out of adjustment	Adjust, overhaul, or replace	144–146
Chain jumps or skips	1. New chain on worn sprocket	Replace sprocket or freewheel	81–83
	2. Chain worn or slack (non-derailleur bike)	Adjust chain tension or replace	77
	3. Stiff or bent chain link	Replace link or chain	77–79
Chain drops off chainring or sprocket	1. Derailleur out of adjustment (derailleur bike)	Adjust derailleurs	86–92
	2. Chain loose or worn (non-derailleur bike)	Adjust or replace chain	77–79
	3. Chainring bent or loose	Straighten or tighten	72
	4. Incorrect chain line	Correct chain line	79
Irregular pedaling movement	1. Crank, bottom bracket or pedal loose	Adjust or tighten	66–76
	2. Pedal spindle or crank bent	Replace	73
Derailleur gears do not engage properly	1. Derailleur out of adjustment	Adjust derailleur	86–92
	2. Derailleur dirty or damaged	Overhaul derailleur	90
	3. Derailleur control lever or cable damaged, corroded or maladjusted	Clean, lubricate, adjust, or replace	87–97
	4. Chain too short or too long	Correct or replace	77
	5. Cable guides or lever attachment loose	Tighten	97
	6. Front derailleur loose or not straight	Tighten and align	91–92

Problem or Symptom	Possible Cause	Required Correction	See Page
Indexed derailleur does not shift properly	1. Cable damaged or corroded	Replace and lubricate	97
	2. Derailleur out of adjustment	Adjust derailleur	87–92
	3. Chain or sprockets worn	Replace	77–83
Hub gearing does not work properly	1. Hub out of adjustment	Adjust hub gear	100–106
	2. Shift lever defective	Clean, lubricate, or replace	104
	3. Control cable pinched or damaged	Free, lubricate, or replace	104
	4. Cable guide loose	Reposition and tighten	104
Rim brake ineffective	1. Brake out of adjustment	Adjust brake	113
	2. Brake pads worn	Replace	111
	3. Rim wet, greasy or dirty	Clean rim	36
	4. Steel rim in wet weather	Replace with aluminum rim	46
	5. Brake cable corroded, pinched or damaged	Free, lubricate or replace cable	125
	6. Brake lever loose or damaged	Tighten, free, lubricate, or replace	120
	7. Wheel seriously out of round	Straighten rim	43–46
	8. Brake loose or bent	Tighten, free, lubricate, or replace	127
Rim brake jitters	1. Brake loose	Tighten mounting bolt	127
	2. Rim seriously out of round	Straighten rim	44–46
	3. Rim dirty or greasy	Clean rim	36
	4. Headset loose	Adjust headset	144
Rim brake squeals	1. Brake pads contact rim poorly	Adjust or bend brake arm	113–118
	2. Rim dirty	Clean rim	36
	3. Brake pads worn or dirty	Replace brake pads	111–118
	4. Brake arms loose	Tighten pivot bolt	121

Problem	Cause	Remedy	Page
Coaster brake ineffective	1. Chain loose	Adjust chain	77
	2. Brake torque arm loose	Attach or tighten	132
	3. Brake hub defective	Overhaul or replace hub	132
Drum brake ineffective	1. Cable or control problems	Free, lubricate, replace	133
	2. Brake torque arm loose	Tighten	133
	3. Brake lining worn or greasy	Reline or exchange brake shoes	133
Stirrup brake ineffective	1. Control rod or lever problems	Check, straighten, lubricate, and adjust controls	126
	2. Brake pads worn or rim damaged	Clean, adjust, replace	111
Conventional battery lighting defective	1. Battery exhausted	Replace battery	166
	2. Battery contact defective	Clean, bend, scrape	165
	3. Contact in lamp housing defective	Repair contact	165
	4. Switch defective	Clean contacts, bend spring	165
	5. Bulb loose or defective	Reseat or replace bulb	165
Rechargeable battery lighting defective	1. Battery exhausted	Recharge or replace battery	166
	2. Battery contact defective	Clean, bend, scrape	165
	3. Wiring contact loose	Repair connection	165
	4. Contact in lamp housing defective	Repair contact	165
	5. Switch defective	Clean contacts, bend spring	165
	6. Bulb loose or defective	Reseat or replace bulb	165
Dynamo lighting defective	1. Dynamo slips off tire	Adjust or bend mountings	167
	2. Bulb loose or defective	Reseat or replace bulb	167
	3. Wiring or contact pad loose	Repair connection	167
	4. Contact in lamp housing defective	Repair contact	167
Accessory inoperable	1. Mounting hardware defective	Tighten or remove	170

Bibliography

Note:

This list includes only bicycle-repair-relevant titles. For a more complete listing of technical titles, consult my book **Bicycle Technology***.*

Barnett, J. *Barnett's Manual.* Brattleboro, VT: Vitesse Press, 1989.

Berto, F. *Upgrading Your Bike. Emmaus, PA: Rodale Press, 1989.*

Coello, D. *The Mountain Bike Repair Handbook.* New York: Lyons & Burford. 1990.

Coles, C. W., H. T. Glenn, J. Allen. *Glenn's Complete Bicycle Manual.* New York: Crown Publishers, 1989.

Cuthberson, T. Anybody's Bike Book. Berkeley, CA: Ten-Speed Press, 1992.

DeLong, F. *DeLong's Guide to Bicycles and Bicycling.* Radnor, PA: Chilton Books, 1978.

Editors of Bicycling Magazine. *Bicycling Magazine's Complete Guide to Bicycle Maintenance and Repair.* Emmaus, PA: Rodale Press, 1986.

Sloane, E. *Sloane's Handy Pocket Guide to Bicycle Repair.* New York: Simon & Schuster, 1993.

Van der Plas, R. *Bicycle Technology.* San Francisco: Bicycle Books, 1992.

———. *Cycle Repair: Step by Step.* Huddersfield (GB): Springfield Books, 1003.

———. *Mountain Bike Maintenance.* San Francisco: Bicycle Books, 1993.

———. *Roadside Bicycle Repairs.* San Francisco: Bicycle Books, 1990.

Stevenson, J. and B. Richards. *Mountain Bikes: Maintenance and Repair.* San Francisco: Bicycle Books, Huddersfield (GB): Springfield Books, 1993

Sutherland, H. *Sutherland's Handbook for Bicycle Mechanics.* Berkeley, CA: Sutherland Publications, 1992.